Penguin Modern European Poets
*Advisory Editor: A. Alvarez*

# Selected Poems · Sándor Weöres · Ferenc Juhász

Sándor Weöres was born in 1913 into a family of small landowners in Western Hungary. He studied law, history, geography and philosophy in the universities of Pécs and Budapest, and has made his living as librarian, editor and translator. His first book of poems appeared in 1934, and chief among his more recent collections are *A hallgátas tornya* (*The Tower of Silence*, 1956); *Tüzkút* (*Well of Flames*, 1964); and *Merülö Saturnus* (*Saturn Sinking*, 1968). He has also published several engaging books of verse for children, and has translated poems from many languages.

Ferenc Juhász was born in Bia, near Budapest, in 1928. He began his studies at Budapest University in 1947, but left and started work with a publisher as a sub-editor. His first volume of poems, *Szárnyas Csikó* (*The Winged Foal*), was published in 1949. In 1950 he was awarded the highest Hungarian literary prize for his 'socialist-realist' epic poem *Apám* (*Father*). In 1953 his book of verse, *Óda a Repüléshez* (*Ode to Flight*), represented a change of mood from realism to a genuine fusion of modernism and folk motives. In 1954 he published his best-known book, an epic poem, *Tékozló Ország* (*Prodigal Land*), about Dozsa, the martyr leader of the 1514 peasant rebellion. After the appearance of his first collected poems in 1956, he did not publish until the sixties. His latest book of verse, *Harc a Fehér Báránnyal* (*Fight with the White Lamb*), appeared in 1965.

# Selected Poems

Sándor Weöres

*Translated with an Introduction by*
Edwin Morgan

Ferenc Juhász

*Translated with an Introduction by*
David Wevill

Penguin Books

Penguin Books Ltd, Harmondsworth,
Middlesex, England
Penguin Books Inc., 7110, Ambassador Road,
Baltimore, Md 21207, U.S.A.
Penguin Books Australia Ltd, Ringwood,
Victoria, Australia

First published by Penguin Books 1970


Made and printed in Great Britain by
C. Nicholls & Company Ltd
Set in Monotype Bembo

# *Contents*

SÁNDOR WEÖRES

*Introduction* by Edwin Morgan 9
Eternal Moment 15
The First Couple 16
The Underwater City 19
To Die 21
Wedding Choir 22
The Colonnade of Teeth 24
Whisper in the Dark 26
The Scarlet Pall 27
Clouds 29
The Lost Parasol 30
Moon and Farmstead 43
Orpheus Killed 44
Queen Tatavane 46
In the Window-Square 51
Rayflower 52
Terra Sigillata 53
In Memoriam Gyula Juhász 55
Signs 57
Internus 59
Mountain Landscape 64
The Secret Country 65
Difficult Hour 67
Coolie 69
Monkeyland 70

FERENC JUHÁSZ

*Introduction* by David Wevill 75

PART 1

Silver 83

Gold 84

Birth of the Foal 85

Then There Are Fish 87

Comet-Watchers 88

Mary 90

The Tower of Rezi 91

November Elegy 93

PART 2

The Boy Changed into a Stag Clamours at the Gate of Secrets 97

PART 3

Hunger and Hate 113

Four Seasons 114

The Flower of Silence 116

A Church in Bulgaria 117

A Message Too Late 122

Black Peacock 123

The Rainbow-Coloured Whale 125

Thursday, Day of Superstition 130

# Sándor Weöres

# *Introduction*

Sándor Weöres is a protean poet of great virtuosity, writing in all forms, from complex metre and rhyme to free verse, keenly aware of the musical and rhythmical powers which poetry shares with song and dance and ritual, and from this delighting in the means which poetry particularly offers of uniting the sophisticated and the primitive. His inventiveness sometimes creates imaginary languages, and phonetic and visual effects similar to those we have seen in many countries in recent years. Not surprisingly, he has a very 'open' view of what poetry is and can do, and has no sympathy with any socio-political prescriptiveness. Exploration and experiment are essential to his art, as he made clear during an interview in 1963:

> Yes, I think one should explore everything. Including those things which will never be accepted, not even in the distant future. We can never know, at the start of an experiment, where it will lead. . . . It may take decades or centuries to prove whether it was a useful experiment or a useless one. It may never be proved at all.*

Poems which are hostages to such far-off verdicts as these may very properly be difficult, or at times even obscure. A bold use of associational imagery is coupled with a wide range of mythological and anthropological reference drawn from India and China, Egypt and Africa and Polynesia; Weöres himself has admitted the influence on him of the Upanishads, the Gilgamesh epic, and the works of Lao Tse. Although he does write about familiar figures, as in the remarkable 'Orpheus Killed', he seems more often to drive

* Interview with László Cs. Szabó, published in *Tri-Quarterly*, Evanston, Illinois, No. 9, Spring 1967.

farther back and out to the least known and the least appreciated, and even to those he will invent for himself, as if it was important to remind modern man, swinging in his cradle of an extraordinary technology, how far his mysterious roots crawl into lost times and places, never quite forgotten and never quite recoverable. So he writes about Adam and Eve themselves in the guise of two imaginary mythological characters, Kukszu and Szibbabi, in 'The First Couple'. The poem ends movingly with a brief, intense encapsulation of our awareness that change is traumatic, and that because this is so we look back with impossible longing to early and superseded stages:

  Kukszu sprawls in scalding mud,
head in silt, feet in sedge,
face turned to the sky,
sends no more blood-rain into the body of Szibbabi,
cries with sharp call, a suckling child,
waiting for the overflowing light, for the overflowing light
waiting, for the never-returning light.

In the long, rich, exotic 'Queen Tatavane', Weöres again uses a series of invented names which are all meant to evoke the strangely isolated, melting-pot anthropology of Madagascar, where the distant Malay and Polynesian voyagers unite with the near-at-hand Africans. The young queen, bound by rituals and obligations she would dearly like to be free of, must rule over her 'two nations', and justify their struggles, trying to bring something new to birth:

Pain of two nations is fire under me,
who will ever hatch the happiness of the world?

Again and again Weöres' poems acknowledge all the archetypal sources of strength, and refuse to reject the primitive. When he uses real names, the most remote analogies and reminders can touch off our responses as readily as do the imaginary figures. In 'The Secret Country', for example, the mesmeric, winding repetitions take us down into the very essence of an Underworld, though E Daj is an actual name for Hell or the Underworld in one of the Polynesian myths. The fact that few readers will be able to distinguish between the real and invented names is Weöres' way of saying that the poet, if not literally a myth-maker, is certainly a willing collaborator with the basic mythopoeic propensities of man, science or no science, history or no history.

In such a poet, it is natural that there should go with all this a deep sense of the interconnexions of human and non-human life. These connexions, felt more strongly by Weöres than the everyday props and ligatures of social institutions and habits, have sometimes given him a reputation for with-drawnness or pessimism that his work as a whole does not in fact show. Yet although he is obviously not writing for a mass audience, his poetry is so sinewy with energy, so ready to break out into wonder or playfulness that its 'black' qualities must be placed in that broader context of abounding creative pleasure. Even the bitter 'Internus', with its unrelieved catalogue of human failings, its Baudelairean nest of disgusts, has its positives; they emerge in the cleansing, purging power of an artist's 'No!', something utterly distinct from the cynically negative positions the consciously reflective social mind might throw up:

> The panic world is baffled at my gate:
> 'Madman! Egotist! Traitor!' its words beat.
> But wait: I have a bakehouse in my head,
> you'll feed someday on this still uncooled bread.

At the end of 'Internus' the poet imagines his death as a return to the great plenum from which everything is continuously poured. In his long poem 'The Lost Parasol', an astonishingly fertile, original, and thought-provoking work, shimmering with rhyme, half-rhyme, and assonance, the process of dissolving back into a plenum is shown step by step over a period of years, entirely natural, mostly explicable, but fundamentally awesome in its revelation of nature as relentless metamorphosis. Yet the poem is human, and touching, in taking as its central object a simple red parasol, left behind in the grass by a girl in love. The slow disintegration of the parasol, blown about by wind and storm, drenched by rain, torn by rocks and branches, invaded by insects, lizards, mice, and birds, its jaunty red faded and smudged, ends with a last flying tuft of fabric poised between sea and sky, swaying in the light of the Theatrum Gloriae Dei. The two lovers have long forgotten it, but the tiny, symbolically assertive flash of scarlet silk, the one man-made thing in that teemingly non-human landscape, has become a part of the nature that they themselves can neither escape from nor forget. The poem's final image is one of joy – the poet sings exultantly like the oriole in the forest, of love, of change, of death. The poem sings out as the red parasol sang out in the grass.

Weöres has a warm intuitive sympathy which is able to work through quite different tones and structures: the visionary brooding and Blakean 'minute particulars' of 'The Lost Parasol', the epigrammatic statements of 'Terra Sigillata', the dark sardonic probing of 'In Memoriam Gyula Juhász', the amusing but cutting pidgin of 'Coolie'. In the interview already quoted, Weöres answered with a simple 'Yes' when he was asked whether he felt 'the same humility towards your fellowmen as Montaigne felt towards the illiterate gardener'. Political regimes come and go (and Weöres has persisted quietly through oppressive periods in the past), but the basic sympathies of an unpolitical poet give his work a humanity which his immense technical gifts and wide reading in no way obscure. Two of the epigrams in 'Terra Sigillata' make the point:

The Dazzling is always coming to earth to beg for mud,
while his palace in heaven, stiff with gold, sighs for his return.

The bowed-down carrier looks up: there he stands at the centre of
  the earth!
it is above his head that the sky's vault goes highest.

Both Christianity and Marxism could be read into these couplets – and also, in the first of them, something more oriental and more deeply revolutionary than either system. Like bread cast on the waters, the poems of Weöres set off into the unknown, swirling into some Jungian E Daj of the mind where it seems as natural to 'come to the earth to beg for mud' as it is, in 'Difficult Hour', to 'lay open the powers of the bodiless inner world'.

EDWIN MORGAN

## *Eternal Moment*

What you don't trust to stone
and decay, shape out of air.
A moment leaning out of time
arrives here and there,

guards what time squanders, keeps
the treasure tight in its grasp –
eternity itself, held
between the future and the past.

As a bather's thigh is brushed
by skimming fish – so
there are times when God
is in you, and you know:

half-remembered now
and later, like a dream.
And with a taste of eternity
this side of the tomb.

## *The First Couple*

'Get up, Kukszu,
up, Kukszu, Kukszu, get up,
take your rod and thrash the trees!'

'I won't get up, Szibbabi, I won't get up,
my head lies heavy in scalding mud, my eyes
are shut, my face looks up to the sky,
I will not take my rod in my hand, Szibbabi, I will not get up,
I am sending blood-red rain on you,
I am staying where I am.'

Szibbabi went off,
when she got to the lake
lifted her apron.

'Lake frog, take a rod,
thrash the trees!'

'I won't thrash, Szibbabi, I won't thrash the trees,
I live with my own true mate,
we hide from the hungry bird,
we eat big mosquitoes day after day.'

Szibbabi let her apron down,
the blood-rain overtook her.

The frog smiled tenderly and said:
'Beyond the lake, beyond the mountains
there are twelve big-navelled gods

so fond of fruit, so fond
of mash, mash made with lard,
and they hold suckling babies in their laps,
and in their hip-bones they hold the world,
in their hip-bones both sky above and earth beneath,
and between these the water runs up and down.'

Szibbabi left
by the lake-side, to get to the mountain,
over the mountain, to get to the twelve gods.
When she'd put the lake behind her
her head broke off from her neck,
rolled back into the lake.
When she'd got to the mountain
her trunk broke off at the waist,
lay there with her two arms.
When she'd found the twelve gods
then her two legs broke off.

The twelve gods smiled tenderly and said:
'You under the waist,
you above the legs,
you sack of skin once called Szibbabi,
let the blood-rain leave you,
may you shut as tight
as shell round ripening seed,
and when the new light spills over
let out your young, be flat again,
become a cracked and juiceless skin,
and let your young be Kukszu.'

Kukszu sprawls in scalding mud,
head in silt, feet in sedge,
face turned to the sky,
sends no more blood-rain into the body of Szibbabi,

cries with sharp call, a suckling child,
waiting for the overflowing light, for the overflowing light
waiting, for the never-returning light.

# *The Underwater City*

Who has no crumbling smoke – who has buried
all her flowers among the sad deaf waves, afraid
of the evil and for its sake shunning the good as well:
coward-city! she stirs my heart.

Instead of the sheet of the sky
the living sheet of seaweed, covering,
moving endlessly, noiselessly, mum as a thousand mice.
Noiseless seaweed music, thinkable music, not for the ear,
bygone city music, once heard by the ear –
musicless in this place the underwater city.

This city too I will throw off, till nothing is left.
Let her swim in the abyss of my past, waving her seaweed-
  cover,
lamenting her flowers and her bygone music.
Her cairn of stones, like knee-pans of scrawny gods,
their hard hip-bones and rasping ribs,
is beyond anxiety: death seizes, fuses everything.
Because I cast even this coward-city off, I want no memories
  of the music either.
Even her melancholy seaweed-cover is too much for me.

And if someone comes and asks me what I have:
what have I gathered in this world among
the monotonous mechanical clatter of nights and days?
what gives me licence to spend or hoard? –
I will show him this city. Rejected infernal city!
Look now: dying stones, flowers desired,

old trembling through the seaweed – such is the underwater city.
Yet I say: this is all you can gather together.
Because there is nothing more anywhere.

## *To Die*

Eyes of mother-of-pearl, smell of quince,
voice like a bell and far-off violins
and hesitant steps hesitating, thickening,
heavy-horned twins of emptiness snickering,
sinking, cold brimming, blue wide over all!
Wide magnet blue, ploughs flashing on,
and burning thorns in naked storm,
earth-wrinkles, dropped on pitted soil,
shaking the wild sweet nest, the bright
dish flying in its steady-spread light.

## *Wedding Choir*

1

Life-filled longing of the buoyant smile strains against
imminent certainty, against the radiant food-bringer.
Brooding between good and evil, it loses bright warmth
  in languor,
slips down blood-red below empty stars, into chequered
  mutilation.
But the white bird of Union flies to it, nestles there,
settles maturely, hugely, in the flashing joy of the message.

2

Flocks of bright fables rise over the spreading scarlet cinders:
dead skeleton and growing body are praised by the grey-
  beard.
A cart, where troubled charm and trancelike beauty warm
  themselves wound into one,
painful and shining, like plunging into sleep: close to the
  cauldron is the feast of the fable.
Kingfisher-flocks fly shrieking: the cry links everything!
the ritual fire flashes: prophecy pours time in its mould.

3

The straining pillar and the dancing fire are obstinate as a
  marriageable girl:
unsignalled instantaneousness, little sailing half-moons,
veiled smile and stunned gladness, fading like the colour
  of flowers,
brilliant caprices that instead of hurting brim over with love.
Long the street, but a thousand lodgings on both sides
  harbour saintly unity.
Seed of all things: clear dignity! and sweet the broken
  fortune piercing the husk.

4

The tense wing crumples, the glimmering laughter burns
out,
shadow looms, and the steady pulse of hunger beats to its
quietus.
Between good and evil, in colourless mist, a dim ripple of
the soul,
the desperate slopes and huddle of stars adrift in it.
The Shining Fish lives, a peace unbroken,
an ambergris-scented order, clothed with imperfection and
salmon-running joy.

# *The Colonnade of Teeth*

1

The Colonnade of Teeth, where you have entered,
red marble hall: your mouth,
white marble columns: your teeth,
and the scarlet carpet you step on: your tongue.

2

You can look out of any window of time
and catch sight of still another face of God.
Lean out of the time of sedge and warblers:
God caresses.
Lean out of the time of Moses and Elias:
God haggles.
Lean out of the time of the Cross:
God's face is all blood, like Veronica's napkin.
Lean out of your own time:
God is old, bent over a book.

3

Head downwards, like Peter on his cross,
man hangs in the blue sky with flaring hair
and the earth trundles over the soles of his feet.
The one who sees
has sleepless eyes he cannot take from man.

4

No sugar left for the child:
he stuffs himself with hen-droppings and finds what's sweet.
Every clod: lightless star!
Every worm: wingless cherub!

5

If you make hell, plunge to the bottom:
heaven's in sight there. Everything circles round.

6

Man lays down easy roads.
The wild beast stamps a forest track.
And look at the tree: depth and height raying from it to
every compass-point;
Itself a road, to everywhere!

7

Once you emerge from the glitter of the last two columns
the cupola your hair skims is then infinity,
and a swirl of rose-leaves throws you down,
and all that lies below, your bridal bed: the whole world –
Here you can declare:
'My God, I don't believe in you!'
And the storm of rose-leaves will smile:
'But I believe in you: are you satisfied?'

## *Whisper in the Dark*

From a well you mount up, dear child. Your head a pyre, your arm a stream, your trunk air, your feet mud. I shall bind you, but don't be afraid: I love you and my bonds are your freedom.

On your head I write: 'I am strong, devoted, secure, and home-loving, like one who wants to please women.'

On your arm I write: 'I have plenty of time, I am in no hurry: I have eternity.'

On your trunk I write: 'I am poured into everything and everything pours into me: I am not fastidious, but who is there who could defile me?'

On your feet I write: 'I have measured the darkness and my hand troubles its depths; nothing could sink so deep that I should not be deeper.'

You have turned to gold, dear child. Change yourself into bread for the blind and swords for those who can see.

# *The Scarlet Pall*

Your first dream – the dream just cradle-born –
two rosy children in naked interlace
eating each other, biting into soft fat flesh.

Second dream: the black sacrifice to your mother.
Lifting the stone lid, and silence out of the dark.

Third dream now: in shadows of furniture, in a corner
friends hanging head downwards in the air like
blinded lamps . . . who knows if they're alive . . .

  Oh how endlessly
dream ripples out, washes in sullen folds,
clashing thread on scarlet ground: dream: star-army!
figures of lightning on the blood-red pall!
  Remember yet:
the spearlike bud bursts from man's groin,
woman's groin unfolds its flower to meet it,
and as a bow touches a fine quivering string
the bud gushes into the offered cirque of petals.
  Remember yet:
you roam over dead plateaux and rock-wrinkles,
you come upon someone buried to the chin in stone,
and both the roamer and the buried one are you yourself.
You stumble clumsily over the protruding head,
but whose is the head that takes the kick of your boots?

  All your dream,
  all mine too:
our child-dreams drink pearls at the same spring.

A heaven of lace on the rust-crusted outposts,
images on the scarlet pall! Branch-writhing dream!

Dance, dance,
swing through the distance:
what an initiation
your childtime night was!
and the cyclops-eye of the world sat on your skull,
a thousand faces flaked to the bone on your cot,
remember yet –

Across time and space
creep, creep to me:
our savage factious hearts have common root in the earth.
Common, what lies in wait for us.
Think: you are walking in smoke. Your eyes are bandaged.
Heat of torches hits you; you are led by the hand.
And soon perhaps, without fear,
you will sacrifice yourself:
the arch of your eye-covering tugs the flame inwards!
No hiding then from your blood-coloured pall!

# *Clouds*

In the mirror of the open window the mirror-cloud drifts facing the cloud. Cupids melt off at its edge, the heavy centre writhes with the lumbering bodies of monsters, a satiny blueness retracts and spreads bitten between gaping rows of beast-fangs. A violet coach flakes off, hurries away into the blue and quickly vanishes: yet it is easy to imagine it galloping there out of sight: gods are sitting in it, or the no-beings of non-being, or the dead we have heard the earth thudding down on and know nothing about any more.

The clouds drift and the mirror-clouds face them; and for anyone watching, nature drifts face to face with thought in the depths of his skull.

# *The Lost Parasol*

I think there is much more in even the smallest creation of God, should it only be an ant, than wise men think.
ST TERESA OF AVILA

Where metalled road invades light thinning air,
some twenty steps more and a steep gorge yawns
with its jagged crest, and the sky is rounder there,
  it is like the world's end;
nearer: bushy glade in flower,
farther: space, rough mountain folk;
  a young man called his lover
  to go up in the cool of daybreak,
they took their rest in the grass, they lay down;
the girl has left her red parasol behind.

Wood shades sunshade. Quietness all round.
What can be there, with no one to be seen?
Time pours out its measureless froth and
  the near and the far still unopened
  and midday comes and evening comes,
no midday there, no evening, eternal floods
that swim in the wind, the fog, the light, the world
and this tangle moves off into endlessness
like a gigantic shimmering silk cocoon,
skirted by wells of flame and craters of soot.

Dawn, a pearl-grey ferry, was drifting
  on its bright herd of clouds,
from the valley the first cow-bell came ringing
and the couple walked forward, head by head;

now their souvenir clings to the shadows,
red silk, the leaves, the green light on it, filtering,
metal frame, bone handle, button:
separate thing from the order of men,
it came home intact, the parasol,
its neighbours rockface and breeze, its land cold soil.

In a sun-rocked cradle which is as massive
as the very first creation itself
the little one lies, light instrument
on the blue-grey mossy timber of a cliff,
around it the stray whistling, the eternal murmuring
of the forest, vast Turkey-oak, slim hornbeam,
briar-thickets, a thousand sloe-bushes quivering,
noble tranquil ranks of created things,
and among them only the parasol flares out:
jaunty far-off visitor whose clothes still shout.

Languidly, as if long established there,
its new home clasps it about:
the rocks hug their squat stonecrops,
above it the curly heliotropes
cat's-tail veronica,
wild pinks push through cage of thistles,
dragon-fly broods on secret convolvulus,
dries his gauze wings, totters out:
so life goes on here, never otherwise –
a chink in the leaves, a flash of blue-smiling skies.

The sea-lunged forest breathes at it
like yesterday, like long ago,
mild smell of the soft nest of a girl.
Shy green woodpecker and russet
frisky squirrel refused to sit on it,

who knows what it hides: man left it;
but a nosy hedgehog comes up to the ledge,
the prickly loafer, low of leg,
like a steam puffer patrols round the rock;
puts heart in the woodpecker tapping at his trunk.

The sun stretches out its muscular rays:
you would expect the bell of heaven to crack.
Broad world – so many small worlds find their place
in you! Through the closed parasol's hills and valleys
an oblong speck moves: an ant that drags
the headless abdomen of a locust with rapt
persistence and effort: up to the bare heights,
down to the folds, holding the load tight,
and turning back at the very end of the way,
floundering up again with the body. Who knows why?

This finger-long journey is not shorter or sillier
than Everything, and its aim is just as hidden.
Look: through the branches you can see the hillside,
there a falcon, a spot on the clear sky,
hangs in the air like a bird of stone:
predator, hanging over from history.
Here, wolf and brown bear were once at home,
crystalline lynx lay in ambush for the innocent.
God wetted a finger, turned a page
and the world had a very different image.

A sky-splitting single-sloped precipice,
its lap a lemon-yellow corrie of sand,
far off a rosy panorama of mist,
curly hills in a ragged mauve cloud-band;
above, the couple stood; below, the sun-wheel
stirred;

in the dawn-flames, so interdependent
they stood, afraid, at the very edge of fate;
boulders rolled from beneath their feet,
    they were quarrelling, tearing their hearts,
each of them deaf before the other starts.

In the tangled thicket of their young blood
the luminous world skulks off, sinks;
    shame like a rose-branch cut
        the boy to the quick:
beyond entreaty, ready to throw himself down to . . .
His white shirt gestured against the blue,
    at the shrubby scarp with its bindweed
        he lurched forward, forward
growing smaller and more distant – and his frightened
            girl
runs after him through briars, her knee's blood is a pearl.

Tall sedges lean over the gorge
and like a gemmed porch of the depths below
an army of tiny shining shields of weeds
    and a thick dark couch of green
cling round the bark of a stump that points no-
where, here their frenzy lost its rage:
they twined together, to ask why, to cry,
like the horned moon the white flash of a thigh;
a hooded boletus at their feet
fattened its spore-crammed belly, not bothering to mate.

        The hilltop sends down
        wind tasting of stone
    to crochet sudden air-lace;
    and the lost parasol
    shivers and half lives;

in the endlessly intricate forest, in the deep maze
of its undergrowth, a breeze
lurks, but takes off at the sharp rock-fall,
pouring over that solitary wall
and across the ravine, flying light to the dale.

Zigzag mane of the thicket
wavers and swirls,
the forest depths are sighing,
a thousand tiny leaves, like birds' tails, flicker
and glint in the light like scales;
drawn up from a breeze-wakened copse
yeasty, spicy fragrances are flying;
a snapped thorn-branch stirs, drops,
catches on the soft fabric:
on the tent-like parasol the first tear is pricked.

No one is sorry –
right above it an oriole is calling,
inside it a bow-legged spider scurries
round and round the scarlet corrie
and makes off: under the metal-arched ribs
a lizard twists in search of his siesta,
he guzzles the oven-heat and like a jester
propped on both hands peeps out from the midst;
later some mice come running in and out
and the shaft has a gaudy tit perking about.

In the vault of summer skies, diamond-blue,
an ice-white lace-mist moves in a smile;
over the plain, at the foothills of heaven,
there are dark woolpacks hanging heavy
and truant cloud-lines in crumbling style;
Apollo, body stripped, striding through,

runs young, strong, and fresh,
hot oil steams on the earth's rough flesh;
in air that rocks both valley and peak,
in empty immensities – a red spot of silk.

The girl of the neglected parasol
is just as small, lost in the broad world,
a tiny insect dropped in a sea-wide flood;
no one to talk to at all,
wrapping her own soul round her fear,
she curls up in a curtained room,
and hears a whipped dog whining there
as if there was no misery anywhere,
no other wound to ache in earth or heaven;
or does he howl for all the pain of men?

Hanging on the sky's arch
at the lower bank
the dusk
is hazy.
The first? How many before? On the lazy
ridge no grass or insect measures it,
neither cuckoo nor cuckoo-spit,
the twilights turn for ever, as created.
At the rock's edge, with forever's speed
the sleek silk vanishes into foaming shade.

Night's victory, yesterday's goodbye:
huge galley in the bay of earth and sky,
floating catafalque of dead Osiris;
scarlet embers fall into saffron high-tide,
peacock of air bends his fan from the heights,
shimmering feathers are roses and night-stocks;
an organ of gold installed in space

opens up all its pipes and lips,
pencils of light-rays spring from the rifts
and stroke the hills while darkness fills their cliffs.

On the foamy crest of foliage
light and shade come knotted together
like the body's pain and pleasure.
Fading now, from its covert, the cuckoo's message,
and the motley unison
of piping, chattering, chirping, splashing
prankishness and passion.
The evening light, that turns dreams on,
bends through the cool slow-surging trees,
gleams in the silvery homespun of twittering beaks.

Each smallest voice is poured
delicately into the quiet;
the nightingale among thorns, like
a plucked metal string
casts a few notes into the wind,
then uncoils one ringing thread
floating and spinning,
then flicks it like a veil, languid,
then bunches it rippling, potent but light,
and it fades: into a bed carved out of quiet.

The western sky is drained
of the late dusk's arching marble veins,
and the lit-up, burnt-out body of the sky
leaves a steep column of smoke,
pierced through by stars as sharp as steel:
pearl-crest of Boötes between waving trees,
Cygnus a cross drifting lazily by,
Cassiopeia with its double dagger, the rope

of the faintly glimmering Milky Way
loosely folding dead black space away.

The valley, a deep arena, rests,
crisscrossed by shadows of slashed buttresses;
in the cirque a buxom Venus dances,
approaches, spins round, offers riches,
dances naked, white as snow, touches
her feet upon the dew-drenched hills,
soft-bodied, plump, with shining curls,
the slippery form is merged in darkness,
avid monsters stare her through and through;
in a swoon she waves goodbye and the curtain snaps to.

Like rows of houses in an earthquake:
great tangle of trees at the wood's edge
stagger and shake;
a green shoot flies up into the whirlwind,
a grindstone shrieking comes from rocky ledge,
the wilderness tosses and groans;
on the cloud-capped hilltop a thin
lighting burns, crackles, cracks,
then the long crisped fires streaming like flax
split above the cliff, a lion's growl at their backs.

The storm flickers through the twigs,
its thousand necks turn and twist,
it wrestles with the stumbling forest,
a writhing timber in its fist,
leathery roots clutch hard,
lightning tingles in the bark,
hundreds of birds crouch and start
in nests that shake them to the heart,
the burning, clammy monster rages still,
the sky, bowed low, seethes around the hill.

Torn-off leaves whirl anywhere,
roots of a gouged beech prod the air;
the parasol has been swept off the rock,
into a bramble-bush, beside a tree-trunk,
the downpour slaps its silk,
it is all smudged now, frayed, and the ribs show.
It is indifferent to its fate – as the hilltop holds
its head without complaint in thunderbolts,
and with the sky huddles low,
and fixed by sticky clouds watches the daybreak glow.

The parasol has a new home:
the secret world in fallen leaves,
cool dark earth and mouldering grove,
pallid trailers, roots in graves,
horrors endless, puffy, ropy, cold,
centipede country, maggot metropolis;
the days swing round like catapults,
casting the full sun over it, the old
weltering moon; and the parasol sprawls
like a flaking corpse, though it never lived at all.

Autumn rustles: stuffs dead leaves in it;
winter gallops: it is all snow;
the thaw sets it free again:
earth-brown, washed-out now.
A sprouting acorn pushes,
and through the slack, loose
fabric a tiny flag
thrusts the fibres back:
green, tender tassel steers to the weathervanes;
a few more years and a tree will shade the remains.

The parasol has changed: it has left human hands;
the girl has changed too: she is the woman of a man;

once, the red sail and the steerer ran
   lightly together, roving free,
while hosts of drunkenly foaming plum-trees
tempted the wasps to stir noisily
   and deep in the girl's heart the bumble-bees
began to swarm and buzz mischievously;
since then, this wild army has been busy,
building a fortress in her woman's body.

   Both man and woman have forgotten it now,
though it was the first witness of their linked fates:
Lombard silk and red Rhine dye,
long-travelled Indian ivory,
Pittsburgh iron, Brazilian wood, how
   many handcarts have trundled its parts,
   they have gone by rail, they have gone in boats:
a world to make it! son of a thousand hands!
yet no curio: old-world frippery;
lost: no joy in that, yet no great misery.

Branching veins draw it into the dark,
   light-unvisited mud weighs it down,
it is mere rags, dying in dribs and drabs,
it has stopped serving exotic demands
and like a bird escaping its cage-door
   takes up its great home:
the dissolving soil, the swirl of space, the rays
draw it all ways, confused, astray,
old shoreless floods map its new phase:
this is creation's first emergent day.

   Neither sun, moon, nor watch
   can measure creation's second and third days:
   the father of vegetation keeps his watch

over it, pumpkin-head, Saturn, dark face
with grey eyebrows hanging to his chin.
Pulsing life-fluid filters in:
powdered cloth, rotten wood, rusted iron
dissolve and disappear in tangle and thorn,
and sucked up slowly by each hair-vein
it seethes alive again in the humming vortex of green.

Its handle is visible through the leaf-mould.
A brown moth settles there, perches awhile.
By midnight it has laid
hundreds of eggs, a mass of tiny balls
placed in smooth strips, finely embroidered.
And like a biblical ancestress
she opens her wings, floats victorious,
queen fulfilled in happiness,
not caring that dawn brings death:
God in the sky drew up my trembling crest!

The parasol no longer exists: bit by bit
it set off into the open world,
all changed, part after part;
even the eyes of Argus might find no trace,
swivelling across the light,
sliding down to the shade;
only a single feeble fibre remains,
poised on the top of a bramble-prickle,
it is mere fluff, next to invisible;
flies up from the thorn-prick, jumps into the saddle

of a storm! Air-pockets toss it lily-thin,
the mountains shift below
in stampede, buffalo trampling buffalo;
fog-blanket opens on dark forest paths,

brooks twinkling down in the shy straths,
sharp drop of the crag wall, a mine,
toy trains of tubs moving along the rails,
scattered homesteads, a town with its smoke-trails,
and overhead, the great bleak acres of silence
and below, the hill from which the tuft went flying.

Upwards, still higher up it floats:
the moon hangs close like a white fruit,
the earth is a round, tilted, blotchy shroud
    framed by blackness and void.
        Bathed in airy juices,
the fluff swings heavy like a full leather bottle,
    descends to the ground, settles:
    on a green plain, in drizzly mists,
it hovers lightly among the acacias
and probes a calf's ear as its resting-place.

    A thunderstorm crashes, carries it off,
flies with it raggedly over moor and bog,
like a spool it turns, winding the fog,
    and when it is all spun onto a distaff:
low blue sea and high blue sky are combers,
    two sun discs gaze at each other
    and between the two blue shells
            a ghostly sail
            sways, tranquil,
uncaring whether it sways in air or swell.

The vapour-tulip throws back its head,
a glass-green other-worldly meadow glistens,
at the horizon a purple thorn gathers;
darkness surrounds the far-off island;
a little ray like a woman's glance flickers,

caresses its fugitive lover, glitters
as it flutters onto its drowsy son,
while a smile dawns eternity on man,
its arches bend and march on their way
between watery shores, Theatrum Gloriae Dei.

* * *

The red silk parasol was my song,
sung for my only one;
this true love is the clearest spring,
I have smoothed its mirror with my breath,
I have seen the two of us, the secret is known:
we shall moulder into one after death.
Now I expend my life exultantly
like the oriole in the tree:
till it falls down on the old forest floor,
singing with such full throat its heart must burst and
soar.

## *Moon and Farmstead*

full moon slip swim
wind fog foam chord hum
the house empty

rampant
thorn fence
eye blaze

moon swim flame
grass chord twang
cloud fling

the house empty
door window
fly up

chimney run
fog swirl
full moon circle

the house empty

## *Orpheus Killed*

I lie in a cold shaded courtyard, I am dead.
I am sobbing over my body, so many women, men.
Grief rolls from the drum and I start dancing. Who
killed me, why?
        I drift round the market, in palaces,
in taverns, among the flute-players, till in drink
I can say to the drunk: Look at me, I am
your hearts: engaged to death for the sake
of beggars and the blind.
        Stone I am and metal I am
on a slave's cross. The corpse is staring wide-eyed,
grief rolls from the drum and I dance. I am everything
and I am nothing: oh, look at me. I am everyone
and I am no one: stone and metal, many shapes,
on a slave's cross. Why did the priests kill me?
Did I slight their temple?
        Dismembered I lie in the wasteland,
what urn is there for my white dust? Why
did the women tear me? Do they want my dead love?

Wolves of the famished earth prowl all round me,
decay rains rolling down and I start dancing.
Cain I am and saint I am: kneel at my feet.
Leper I am and clean I am: touch me. Body
moves, weak joints crack, cold tears trickle, he
sweats, sweats. Mindless I am and wise I am,
ask no questions, understand in silence. Dead I am
and alive I am, a dumb face, I. A wax-face
sacrifice turns skyward, ringed by staring horror, grief
rolls from the drum and I dance.

No asking back
the body stretched on the cross. I lie harvested in the wasteland,
no asking back the grain laid up in barns.
Death's drum rolls, I whirl in the dance for ever,
the song flooding the valley refreshed by my blood,
my secret endless life entangled in the groves of death.

## *Queen Tatavane*

O my winged ancestors!
Green branch and dry twig you gave me
for my two empires, to plant one and to lash one.
I am small as a weasel, pure as the eastern Moon,
light-ankled as a gazelle, but not poised for flight –
my heart lies open to you, to every silent suggestion.

The Elephantstar took my fifteenth year,
the Dragonstar brought this, the sixteenth.
I am allowed three husbands by ancestral decree
and seven lovers beneath the holy jasmine-leaves.

Not for me to escape with girl-friends to the fields,
for happy laughter, goats to milk, fresh milk to drink,
instead I sit on the throne in your light year after year,
an ebony idol with the world's weight on my neck.

Negro caravans, Arab ships are my traffic and merchandise,
I pay well, though I see most as polecats and monkeys,
but even the sky rains on unchosen ground, seeds burst unchosen.
I survey the naked hosts lost in their prison,
all of them I love as if they were my children,
punishing them with the rod and if need be by the sword,
and though my heart should bleed my looks are frozen.

Wake up, my fathers and mothers! Leave the ash-filled urn,
help me while the mists crawl;
your dark little daughter pleads with you as the last queen,
waiting among the garlands of the cedar-hall.

My seat among stone lions, the man's throne empty at my
side,
my brow is glowing ruby-wreathed like the dawn-clouds,
my purple-tinted fingers, my drowsy almond eyes
shine like a god's as they strike down and raise;
what you found sweet and bitter I come to, I taste.

Orange veils on my shoulders, fireflower wreaths on my
dark hair,
the reedpipe cries, the eunuchs drone, the altar's set.
Come Bulak-Amba my starry bull-browed ancestor!
Come Aure-Ange my lovely holy milk-rich ancestress!

Mango, areca, piled on the altar,
the year's brimming rice, brown coconut, white copra,
all round, red flower thrown on red flower,
sweet sandalwood fumes float up into the air.

Great man-spirit with no name: eat!
Great woman-spirit with no name: eat!
Huge emptiness in the silence behind the drumbeat: eat!

I call you, my father over the foam,
my old begetter, Batan-Kenam,
you are coming in your sun-chariot, four-elephant-drawn,
through the head-waving rattlesnakes of five cosmic storms,
my soldier, ageless, coral-garlanded,
blue-shirted arms,
lance of sky's shark-bone, turtle shield,
cut-off locks of the seven dancer-stars shimmer at your belt,
your elephants lumber and stamp, tiger-herds are felled,
and you rest on your elbow at the world's end in the lee of
the loud blue mountain –
I salute you my glittering visitor, my far-off father!

I am wrapped in my veil, I am hidden,
the welcoming hostess is timid,
I hand out half-peeled oranges on a gold dish:
look at me here, I am your own flesh,
you know I am supple and clawed like a forest cat,
you pause if you see my dark green shining eyes,
my white-hot teeth-embers,
behind, my skeleton is lace-fine, a dragon-fly:
see your one-day-old woman! one smile is all she would
wish!

I summon you Aruvatene, my mother!
I call you. I am your daughter. Do you love her?
Your little one, will you be her protector?
Look, Nightqueen, at your tiny drop of dew:
the sparkling skin, the swelling breast!
You thick-starred heavenly palm-tree, I dance for you.

Blow the pipe, roll the drum,
my dance-wind skims about you, let it come!
my silver ankle-jangle chatters – from you it came!
my orange shawl flies out – you gave it my name!

But if your beautiful face goes ashy as mist
I give you my blood to drink from your ancient chalice,
turn back, I leave you in peace,
eat, drink in silence.

Come too, Andede, good grandmother,
you are as old as the wind
that snuffles in the oven-cinders.
I shall never be so old,
fugitive with blowing flowers.

Andede, good grandmother,
you are as wrinkled as the stone
that snaps off from the mountain.
I shall never be so wrinkled,
I am the rock-escaping fountain.

Andede, good grandmother,
you smile like a yellow desert place
grinding its bones, toothless sand-cascades
skirting the cosmic border.
That is not my smile,
I am the lady of two empires,
sword and bread on my lap together
under the trickle of my tears.

Andede, good grandmother,
you champ and smack like the green dragon
that swallows up the wildest moor.
But I can never be satisfied,
two nations fight to eat from my hand
and bread forever lusts after sword.

Andede, good grandmother,
perpetually decaying, never destroyed,
you are puny but sinewy like a root in the earth,
I am the mother of everybody,
I would take them all on my lap,
I would let them all eat and sup,
but when I even raise my hand, I die.

Great man-spirit with no name: eat!
Great woman-spirit with no name: eat!
Huge emptiness in the silence behind the drumbeat: eat!

Come forward, now, great, ancient, unforgotten,
every sky-dome-breasted queen,
every lightning-dashing king!
I know that your good
is our only food,
but if misery surges again,
here I am – my blame alone,
I your shadow, your orphan,
prostrate under your cane,
beg for that bastinadoing!

For heaven's sake help me then!
Oh I am the virgin peahen
who instead of living eggs
found redhot stones between her legs
and with anxious wings spread wide
broods to hatch a void.
Pain of two nations is fire under me,
who will ever hatch the happiness of the world?

# *In the Window-Square*

In the window-square
*a star* clots
on black sky
dull light forms a minute
the trees surge darkly
distant sea sings in leaves
outside your tight-shut minutes
your star tears you away
the infinite flows and foams through the garden
but in this room space is concentrated
drowns in angle and bay
on red slopes of the armchair
stretches transparently
on the tendril-blue neck of the ewer
flies up to stay
your ring on the table
inextinguishable candle
night slaps the island
hear the sea lapping
things in their deaf shells
clotting in the window-frame
grief hangs over a deep
you picture-book of the universe
in full-lighted age-old existence
shut now at a touch
but my eye runs over the cover
as this star wanders
with its light-year rays
with its blank shoreless gaze

## *Rayflower*

Rayflower
about the head
so flickery
then fled

Above the shoulders
below the chin
a lonely night-light
is carried in

In front of the chest
lace-foam flying
already the fire there
fading dying

In the swelling
of the belly
a shadow spreads
enormously

In a dark sea
no foot lingers
fearing to leave
the lucifer fingers

# *Terra Sigillata*

*Epigrams of an ancient poet*

Useless interrogation: I know nothing. An old man fallen
 asleep,
I wake as a baby, and you can read your learning from my
wide blue eyes; I only glimpse it in recidivist streams.

*

A red-fingered child pats grey cakes at the seaside,
I ask for one, he says no, not even for a real cake, no.
Well now, old prophets, what do you want from me? the
 twenty-four
sky prisms, when I look blind into hearts and read them.

*

If you want your fortune, I'll reel off your identity, your
 expectations,
but I'm deaf to my own words – no plundering secrets.

*

'You say you're God's offspring: why do you scrape along
 like paupers?'
'Even Zeus himself, when he takes human steps on earth,
begs bread and water, parched, starved as a tramp.'

*

The Dazzling is always coming to earth to beg for mud,
while his palace in heaven, stiff with gold, sighs for his
 return.

*

The bowed-down carrier looks up: there he stands at the centre of the earth!
it is above his head that the sky's vault goes highest.

*

Beautiful the lonely pine, beautiful the bee-wreathed rose,
beautiful the white funeral, most beautiful through all – their union.

*

The treasures of a tree! Leaves, flowers, fruits.
How freely it gives them, clinging to the elements alone.

*

The forest has modesty, the wolf hides his death in the shadows,
but a bought mourner will shrill without shame at a stranger's burial.

*

The swindler doesn't slip up with his bogus balance-sheets when his heart is firm,
but when bursting out crying and taking pity on the innocent.

*

Crime has majesty, virtue is holy; but what is the troubled heart worth?
There, crime is raving drunk and virtue is a jailer.

*

The moment I slice the cocoon of my fate: my skull is the sky-dome,
fate-shuttling stars scuttle across its arch.

## *In Memoriam Gyula Juhász**

Let the beasts whine at your grave my father
whine at your grave
let the beasts whine
between the byre and the blade
between the slaughterhouse and dunghill
between the clank of the chain and desolation
my mother as Hamlet said
let the old hunchbacked women whine
between the hospital and the glad rags
between the asylum and the lily-of-the-valley
between the cemetery and the frippery
and the wretches with buried ulcers
between stately doctors and strapping priests
all those paralysed by deferred release
on the far side of hope on the near side of confrontation

Let butterflies twist above the stream
Ophelia who drowned before we were born
the roseless thorn is yours
the profitless pain
the lacklustre ghost in a mourning frame
the falling on knees face in the mud
the humiliation boundless and endless
the dead body without a cross
the unredeemed sacrifice
the hopelessness that is for ever hopelessness

Let rabid dogs howl at your grave
let hollow phantoms hoot

*Hungarian poet, 1883-1937.

my starry brother my bearded bride
the good is only a moment's presentiment
evil is not eternal malice
in the meantime blood flows
lacerated life cannot die
death is deathless liberty

## *Signs*

I

The whole world finds room under my eyelid.
God squeezes into my head and heart.
This is what makes me heavy.
This is what makes the donkey I sit on unhappy.

II

Heaven's crazy-man: light: you
pouring your face on the surface of the water,
what is that girl's face you proffer
stripping from your own madness?

Great saint, having swum through this world
you came to the empty silence, endlessness,
you climbed with the void to a crystal wedding-dress:
be frank, what woman is it like?

III

Man, waken the secret woman in you;
woman, light up your masculine state:
for if the Invisible embraces you,
it will enter you and take you into it.

IV

Oh how large then is love
if it goes with us in our whirlpools?
And what large love lies waiting in us
if it can be taken into our whirlpools?

V

More than your heart's cloudy afflictions,
more than your mind's labour of doubt –

value your toothache more than that,
for its energies.

Words alone can answer your questions,
but each thing answers itself.

## Internus

### Growing Old

My brain's gutterings unwind,
its light – that poverty of mind –
keeps drawing in its radius,
keeps glowing in still dimmer space;
with God's help, I shall hardly see
how far off the cell-wall may be.

### Self-Portrait with Dog

The man I was is dying, his gasps are faint:
the heart is like a stone that stops the throat.
The life-spark, to get back its breath, leaps out
at long last from the miserable body
into a dog, to find tranquillity.
I lay my head down on my master's foot.
I don't feel his pain, I don't remember. I don't.

### Dissolving Presence

It's not my self that interests me,
only that my death, so certain,
saves me from unwanted clowning,
though a tramped-on worm can hurt me.
Is dying going into nothing?
No more despair, no more desire.
But after-life may be no plaything?
I can endure from fire to fire.
Life and death don't interest me,
I only need that harmony
which matter cannot even bear
or reason take into its sphere.

## *Double-faced*

My self: though this perpetual guest
is hardly boring company,
he's a tick to bite my privacy,
without him I'd have quiet and rest.
Because he's attentive to my demon
and shapes its early hints in words
I put up with his earthy being
till evening ends, not afterwards.

## *Out of the Inner Infinity*

From inward infinities I still look out
now and again, seeing through my face
clouds or the winking lights of stars in space.
My eyesight fails, that leaves me like the rest,
the outside world has shut my gates, I'm left
where there is no earth left, but only sky;
and no event, no grace and no surprise,
no surface, nothing seen, no nebulas,
only reality at peace and luminous,
boundless and measureless and nameless,
a love that's still desireless and still changeless.
The panic world is baffled at my gate:
'Madman! Egotist! Traitor!' its words beat.
But wait: I have a bakehouse in my head,
you'll feed someday on this still uncooled bread.

## *The Muddy Drink is Going Down and the Bottom of the Glass Shows Through*

After death shall I still exist?
No handcuffs then upon my wrist,

I have dissolved identity,
why wish it in eternity?
Being or non-being: nakedness
suits undying presences.

I never thought it could be so:
my body gasps for its last breath,
yet still and easy is my soul.
My life is wantless and unwanted,
a beggar going on undaunted,
even by my death unhaunted,
with losses and with gains untaunted.
Fate is too kind! I had best not
die this way, like a dying god,
a smiling victory well flaunted;
I should be pulled up by the root
with a cowardly last shout
and get the real end of a man,
not judged for what I solely am.

*Nocturne*

Bored with my being, unutterably,
boxed in male bones perpetually,
I'm given no rest from his presence,
he and I are old bed-fellows,
I can feel his warmth, his sweat,
from his hair-roots to his feet,
feel the twistings of his bowels,
his man's-stump and his milkless nipples,
the wheezing of his lung-bellows,
his heart-beats on uneasy pedals,
his gnawing and his stabbing pains,
his lusts that break the lagging reins,

his times of hunger and of thirst,
his filled-and-emptied bag of dust,
and what he feels and thinks within
I feel and think, unmoved, with him.
In beastly body-warmth I lie
stuck to a drumming rancid sty.
His daytime braying makes me sick
like his dead snoring, I can't stick
his senses' narrow window-glass,
the wooden O of his mind, a mass
of memories, symbols parroted
hand in hand and madly led.
I'm sick of dandling, pampering him,
of wiping the tarry rump of him,
of taking in his hungry cares,
of making his head utter prayers;
I've been his patient unpaid slave,
caring nothing for what I gave.
Not executioner, but guard,
I hold him close, but killing's barred:
he will die someday just the same,
die in peace or die in pain.
Each cell and seed he has, in its fervour
would go on fucking and gorging for ever,
and the pitiful keen-kindled mind
for ever have new knowledge to find,
but clenched in vice of flesh, I stiffen
in cramps of an enclosing coffin.
His life and stir are my own death,
and I fly on his final breath
into the love of God, fly back
till I'm a stitch in nothing's sack
and need no longer share my soul
or body with my self at all,

being unbounded plenitude,
the latency not understood
who taking all things into him
pours his wealth from a stintless brim.

## *Mountain Landscape*

Valley brook
birdsong squabble.

High quiet
home of god-faced
rocks hanging.

And higher, Nemo's song,
hilltop grindstone-squeal:
ice cracks smart.

## *The Secret Country*

One day we'll jump on a floating log, E Daj the distant is
waiting for us,
we'll float on the log, wing-locked butterflies,
dance gently downwards through the traveller's-joy
beneath the sea, no one aware of us.

Below earth and sea there is a black lake,
motionless and mirror-sharp,
no one knows its chasms:
E Daj the distant is waiting for us,
one day we'll jump on a floating log, plunge in.

The old men say:
As long as we live,
everything we see
hangs in that mirror in the lake,
our faces, our figures
figured facing down.
The palms, the lianas, the foxes, the stars
all hang there in the mirror of the lake.

Short-lived the butterfly, but it visits the old farmhouse,
puttering about it with its whispering
wings, we hear them whispering,
we run, run into the house.
We don't speak to it, we don't speak to shadows.
It knocks at the door, knocks and knocks, breaks off, goes
back home,
E Daj the distant is waiting for us.

The old men say:
Our faces and figures are reflected in the black lake,
no one sees its depths:
whatever is, was once in them,
whatever was once in them, falls back there,
and this is the eternal return.

The man throws his spear, bends his bow,
the woman scrapes a hole for the fire,
all look for handholds, build huts:
and this is how we live, hanging head down in the mirror of
the lake,
one day we'll jump on a floating log, plunge in.
We can't see what lies below. E Daj the distant is waiting
for us.

# *Difficult Hour*

Time for black prophecies is over: the Winter of History is whistling around us.

Man, with suicidal power in his limbs, poison in his blood, craziness in his head like a mad dog: nobody can see his destiny.

If he wants to scarify people to the bone with his new instruments of devastation: his only attainments are loss of the wheel and of fire, forgetfulness of speech, life on all fours.

But let him extricate himself: let him give up his myriad maggot-teeming acts of idiot self-will, his termite provision-activities for the outer world: first let him measure and order the inner world.

Familiar and ordered inner worlds outgrow individual greed, learn to rub along with one another, even to be in harmony with their outer world.

This is the old practicable way. Up till now, the blood-stained currents of history may have moved with beauty and grandeur but moved to a common death, or worse, narrowed their streams to the further agony of a relentless dehumanization.

But today some cradle rocks a fire-baby bringing divine gifts such as we hardly saw in our dreams.

And just as in bygone days they laid open the secret strength of the material world: they will begin now to lay open the powers of the bodiless inner world.

In the hands of these children the lamp of reason does not dictate, but serve: shining through subconscious life-forces and supraconscious spirit-forces alike, illuminating them and setting them to work in turn.

It was always others man conquered in the past; but – oh tremulous hope! – in the future he conquers himself, and fate subdues itself before him, and the stars.

## *Coolie*

Coolie cane chop.
Coolie go
    go
      only softly-softly
 Rickshaw
 Car
 Dragon-carriage
Coolie pull rickshaw.
Coolie pull car.
Coolie pull dragon-carriage.
      only softly-softly
Coolie go foot.
Coolie beard white.
Coolie sleepy.
Coolie hungry.
Coolie old.
Coolie bean poppyseed little child
big wicked man beat little Coolie.
      only softly-softly
 Rickshaw
 Car
 Dragon-carriage
Who pull rickshaw?
Who pull car?
Who pull dragon-carriage?
Suppose Coolie dead.
Coolie dead.
Coolie no-o-o-o-t know dead!
Coolie immortal
      only softly-softly

# *Monkeyland*

Oh for far-off monkeyland,
ripe monkeybread on baobabs,
and the wind strums out monkeytunes
from monkeywindow monkeybars.

Monkeyheroes rise and fight
in monkeyfield and monkeysquare,
and monkeysanatoriums
have monkeypatients crying there.

Monkeygirl monkeytaught
masters monkeyalphabet,
evil monkey pounds his thrawn
feet in monkeyprison yet.

Monkeymill is nearly made,
miles of monkeymayonnaise,
winningly unwinnable
winning monkeymind wins praise.

Monkeyking on monkeypole
harangues the crowd in monkeytongue,
monkeyheaven comes to some,
monkeyhell for those undone.

Macaque, gorilla, chimpanzee,
baboon, orangutan, each beast
reads his monkeynewssheet at
the end of each twilight repast.

With monkeysupper memories
the monkeyouthouse rumbles, hums,
monkeyswaddies start to march,
right turn, left turn, shoulder arms –

monkeymilitary fright
reflected in each monkeyface,
with monkeygun in monkeyfist
the monkeys' world the world we face.

# Ferenc Juhász

# *Introduction*

Ferenc Juhász was born in 1928, in the village of Bia in western Hungary. His family were peasants. He grew up as part of this peasant community of village and farm, and moved to Budapest in 1945. There he studied art, and began writing poetry. His earliest collections, published in 1949 and 1950, won him much prestige and the important Kossuth Prize. To many at this time, Juhász seemed to embody the spirit of Petöfi, the great nineteenth-century poet of Hungary: the same sweeping, epic talent, an awareness of the aspirations of the Hungarian people. But as events changed in Hungary and in Juhász' personal life, the poems became more intense, more self-involved: a dialogue between the poet and the wilderness he filled with prehistoric creatures, proliferating flowers, mythical birds, and a sense of disconnexion, bewilderment, strain. 'In the years 1957–8 I could not work. Many questions troubled me, besides I was ill for a long time. I thought, I have to begin everything again . . . even the language has to be made new.'

Juhász has written more than any Hungarian poet of his time. His poetry is very uneven, and his energy is colossal. His poetry comes from the grass roots of Hungary: the peasant traditions of folk-tale and ballad, superstitions, the cycle of life and death. He has a child's eye for nature; a mare with her newborn foal:

> And the foal slept at her side,
> a heap of feathers ripped from a bed.
> Straw never spread as soft as this.
> Milk or snow never slept like a foal.

And in 'Comet Watchers' he describes how the entire village rushes out to watch the phenomenon in the sky:

> Over the hill, the star-freaked sky
> blazed brighter than burning hay –
> a stallion with wings and a diamond mane,
> a mane of fire, a streaming tail of blood.

There is an affinity between Juhász and Marc Chagall, a 'natural wonder'. But a poet's world is not so hermetic as a painter's, and as Juhász begins more and more to look around him, his poetry becomes darker. On a visit to a church in Batak, where 4,000 Bulgarians were slaughtered by the Turks nearly a hundred years ago, he is reminded of man's struggle against oppression, and asks:

> What happened here? What does this crying emblem
> mean, here in the heart of the church this once –
> soul and marrow-gifted crown?
> It mourns the madness of power, greed, pride – and the dignity
> of defiance, passion of man and woman,
> for you, you earth, the fiery unquenchable core in us
> Liberty!

The poem, with its refrain 'bone, vertebra, skull', is a cry against violence and tyranny, and is Juhász' own cry of defiance, his attempt to state his role as a poet. The poem is written at white heat, condemning the 'human pig-killing', the 'blood-guzzling' that could happen again if people let it and the exalted sanctuary of the mind, the church, become a 'stone coffin'.

> Bones, vertebrae, skulls . . . enough.
> Can my senses still live with this sight,
> this heaped imagery of horror?
> Is there one cell left in my body
> which hasn't suffered the death these bones did?
>
> Is there a cell in my brain
> that isn't part of this grandeur now?

Have you an ounce of shame left,
poet? Shame for yourself
as you stand here, in a white shirt, a summer suit,
on the stones of this church in August '52?

This poem, 'A Church in Bulgaria', was a declaration and turning point for Juhász. Not overtly a political poet, involved in his own imaginary world, his poems nevertheless begin to reflect his own mood and the mood of the country, as he feels it, more and more. Following Bartók and Zoltán Kodály, he goes back to the ballads and folklore of Hungary, to a deeper vision of Hungary, away from the apparent futility of the present, the emptiness he writes of in 'November Elegy' –

My mind hunts in circles, sober, ruthless and cold.
The dull tapping of autumn rain numbs the soul ...

where he talks about his 'stunted dreams' of 'revolutions not fought', and is reminded of his isolation, his sleeplessness –

... And even if
sleep comes, will tomorrow waken anything?

In this poem, and in 'The Seasons', a personal lament written during his wife's illness, there is despair. But the fertility, the noticing things, the involvement with man, animal and flower, is still there. Juhász' fertility often leads to chaos. Many of his poems are wild, organic growths that get out of hand. No detail escapes his attention. What the gardener plants he becomes part of, gets carried away with. But from this nexus have come some remarkable poems.

The greatest of these, perhaps, is 'The Boy Changed into a Stag Clamours at the Gate of Secrets'. The poem is a long allegory whose form and theme have roots in Hungarian folklore, although it is an entirely original creation. It is a poem of two voices. The mother, alone in her old age, calls out to her son to return, tries to lure him back with pleas and motherly promises. But the son has been turned into a stag: he can't return now; if he did, he would destroy her and desecrate his father's grave. Their voices arc back and forth across the poem, calling, answering each other. The mother's world is the home, the stag's world is the forest: the forest of the past and the technological 'stone forest' of the future. He stands 'on the crest of all time', at the 'gate of secrets', from which there's no turning back except in death, where he and his mother will be joined:

Then you can lay me out in my childhood home,
with your age-veined hands you can wash my body,
close my eyelids, swollen glands, with kisses.
    And when the flesh falls off me,
and the stench it was sweetens to flowers,
    I'll be a foetus drinking your blood,
I'll be your little boy again . . .

'The Stag' has affinities with Bartók, particularly the *Cantata Profana*. The structure and rhythms of the poem derive to some extent from the *regös*-lays, the shaman-songs of ancient Hungary, where there is a magical creature called the Sun Stag who resembles the magic lamb in the ballad 'Fair Maid Julia':

It carried the sun and moon between its horns,
It carried the sparkling star on its brow.
On its two horns were Ay! two fine gold bracelets,
Ay! at its sides were two fine burning candles,
As many as its hairs, so many the stars upon it . . .

who in turn resembles the stag in Juhász' poem:

Each branch of my horns
is a coil of gold rings
each twig of each branch

is a candlestick cluster
each fang-sharp tip
is a fine funeral candle . . .

which, as the poem develops, becomes:

each prong of my antlers a twin-legged pylon
each branch of my antlers a high-tension wire . . .

'The Stag' is the finest example of Juhász' use of folk tradition and ballads to create an original allegory that is both personal and universal. It is a total creation that carries all its levels of meaning along with it: the past to which one can never return, but to which one must return in order to find meaning in the present and strength to go beyond. It is where Juhász cuts himself adrift from the powers and certainties he relied on in the past. Like the poem 'The Rainbow-Coloured Whale', addressed to the grave of his father, it is a summation and farewell:

Life here is peaceful
without you.
Flower then, flower into
the death-wish of the lily.

Juhász is a poet at odds with his time. His weapons are not irony, allusion or insinuation, but energy, imagination, and a passionate 'Hungarian-ness' that he gets from his peasant background. His poetry shows very little literary influence, none of the fashions or styles of the time: he is a native product, touched by surrealism perhaps, whose real roots are in the ballads and folk-songs of Hungary. His own vision of Hungary, with which he identifies himself, isolates him from the 'huge merry-go-round' of the neon world he sees developing around him where, in the city on a rainy night, he sees the 'neon monsters', the beasts of the past return:

A bestiary
of red, blue, green and yellow faces . . .

– a world where man walks alone, where it is 'not permitted' to cry out or complain:

> Where am I going?
> What song am I singing?

Juhász is disillusioned with man's ability to accept substitutes, the artificial – to accept them until reality comes, unrecognized, and destroys him. He has tried to create his own mythology, to express an elemental vision, a totality however chaotic, to set against the world of statistics, paper forms and evasions. His enormous body of poetry is uneven. But he's written some of the finest poems of his time. Speaking out for himself and, one feels, for Hungary, he ends this last poem, 'Thursday, Day of Superstition':

> Hell-bent on life, like a sponge, I head for home
> in the red, green and blue rain: in the age of socialism.

This selection of Juhász' poems was chosen by Flora Papastavrou and myself. I do not know Hungarian, and these translations could not have been done without Mrs Papastavrou's insight, imagination and enthusiasm. She did the roughs, and unlocked many of the poems for me by her interpretations and suggestions; so it was a joint effort. I would like to thank István Siklós, who read the manuscript, made suggestions, and provided me with notes. And also the National Translation Center, Austin, Texas, whose grant helped me to go on with the work.

DAVID WEVILL

# *Part 1*

# *Silver*

The traveller stands in the freezing cold
surrounded by drowsy old men.
His moustache is ice, his eyelashes
inhuman half-moons of silver.
He stands watching the horses,
the snow dusting under their hooves
like a cloud of millions of comets
misting the milky star-roads.
His ears are silver, his hair is silver.
The horses twitch their manes and tails.
Silver the velvet nostrils, the steaming flanks.

## *Gold*

The woman touches her bun
of thinning hair. She laughs,
and drops a spoon and a hunk of bread
in their reaching, grubby hands.
Like roses divining water
the circle of thin red necks
leans over the steaming plates;
red noses bloom in the savoury mist.

The stars of their eyes shine
like ten worlds lost in their own light.
In the soup, slowly circling
swim golden onion rings.

## *Birth of the Foal*

As May was opening the rosebuds,
elder and lilac beginning to bloom,
it was time for the mare to foal.
She'd rest herself, or hobble lazily

after the boy who sang as he led her
to pasture, wading through the meadowflowers.
They wandered back at dusk, bone-tired,
the moon perched on a blue shoulder of sky.

Then the mare lay down,
sweating and trembling, on her straw in the stable.
The drowsy, heavy-bellied cows
surrounded her, waiting, watching, snuffing.

Later, when even the hay slept
and the shaft of the Plough pointed south,
the foal was born. Hours the mare
spent licking the foal with its glue-blind eyes.

And the foal slept at her side,
a heap of feathers ripped from a bed.
Straw never spread as soft as this.
Milk or snow never slept like a foal.

Dawn bounced up in a bright red hat,
waved at the world and skipped away.
Up staggered the foal,
its hooves were jelly-knots of foam.

Then day sniffed with its blue nose
through the open stable window, and found them –
the foal nuzzling its mother,
velvet fumbling for her milk.

Then all the trees were talking at once,
chickens scrabbled in the yard,
like golden flowers
envy withered the last stars.

## *Then There Are Fish*

Forever confusing smoke with weeds,
clouds and sky with water.

Born with no lungs, just a blister
floating in a cage of splinters,
listless fins and hyperthyroid eyes.

Even the smallest fry
chase their hunger as boldly as carp –
mouths, nostrils, eyes
burst on a rising scream like a shoal of bubbles.

A world of nothing but water!

Houses and trees
float up like giant bubbles.

## *Comet-Watchers*

One blind-calm summer night
someone tapped at the window of our house –
'Come out! Come out!
There's a miracle! There, in the sky!'

We jumped out of bed. What is it?
Some secret message from the stars?
I grabbed my mother's hand, it was warm,
I felt her heart beat in my palm.

Barefooted, in shirts and underpants
the whole village gathered out there in the cold;
scared old women, sleep-white faces
frozen in the white light of another world.

The poor came crowding into the street.
Women crossed their arms over their breasts.
Their knees shook as they gaped at the sky –
a fairy-tale, a holy prophecy!

Over the hill, the star-freaked sky
blazed brighter than burning hay –
a stallion with wings and a diamond mane,
a mane of fire, a streaming tail of blood.

I gripped my mother's hand like roots.
I remember the warmth of her body still,
and father pointing up at the horse
blazing away in the fires of its own sweat.

Proudly it flew away over the roofs.
We stood, still as gravestones in its fierce light.
The sky was much darker when it had gone.
O fate of comets, will o' the wisp, our hope!

## *Mary*

Like a little cow swollen with calf
she moons around the field, cow-eyed and staring.
The moon's silver belly hangs low in the sky,
the moon beginning to ebb, and the seas
ebbing with the moon.
She remembers the horde of children
locked in their room, shouting, their faces
pushed between the window-bars,
heads poking out to spy on the world,
red eyelids, petals of blood-red rose.
She loiters slowly away
like a little cow swollen with calf,
her rump swaying as she ambles along.
Above her the stars shine hard and cold.
Her heart-beats are too loud . . .
she doesn't understand . . . she stops,
looks down at her belly, and feels
the little feet kicking like a heart.

## *The Tower of Rezi*

I sit here in the Rezi tower
under a massing of swallows –
through my fieldglasses I follow
their soaring, darting flight.

Below me the yellow harvest land,
poplars and mown fields;
the old forests shedding their leaves,
mist melting distance.

My eyes are glassy stalks,
they catch a swallow as it dips.
It is held in the glasses' lens,
trapped, in a fairy-tale glass tower.

The wonder of this magic spell –
modern wizardry!
It flies so near it's as if
its wings would flit through my pupils.

Inside me now: it dips and dives,
curves, wheels, flutters, drops
(through my body) so lightly,
drunker and drunker with the wind.

I can feel the flutter of lungs,
the ounce of heart's motor –
rib-cage, feather, tail –
lawgivers of the flight's arc.

And I'm flying – it's me, not the bird!
the wonders this lens can do!
The self swirling and dipping
forgets it is only watching.

I'm a spiralling, tiny
swallow now. O you swallows!
I'm hurried aloft and held in the arms
of endless space.

My heart has become a bird,
put on feathers, grown wings –
I share
the soaring infinity of the bird.

Most wonderful, wonderful flight!
Joy, pain, sweetness, tears.
The circling heart feels no boundaries,
each curve brings it nearer to heaven.

And I know, what traps it too
is the huge eye of the lens
(for it wants to escape) – already
its beak makes signals of distress.

Then suddenly, in a careless moment
it breaks from the path of the lens –
swallow, where are you? Heart?
Torn clean away with the rest of the swallow-flock.

Through the fieldglasses I search
blue nothingness.
Nothing but the infinite there.
What happened? Am I left with no heart?

# *November Elegy*

My mind hunts in circles, sober, ruthless and cold.
The dull tapping of autumn rain numbs the soul.
Rain drips from the ivy leaves
in heavy, sticky threads: earth, sky, the roof-eaves
sweat with fever. Soon there'll be nothing alive!
I can't sleep, my mind has lost its wings.
My brain is a live coal, the bedclothes are flames
eating my bones. Ships' horns
cry from the Danube. The light from the street is sick,
it throws ghostly leaves on the wall, and tricks
the still, painted horses in my friend's
picture – whinneying, they dance from their frame.
I put my arm around you, your touch soothes me.
Under my hand your breathing is poetry,
pulse, rhythm, ebb, flow, the heart's knocking.
But sleep won't come, the rhythm's lame, and shies away –
the clear voice of sleep can't sing
my stunted dreams: of revolutions not fought,
memories, fevers, desires that swirl in the heart's
bottomless slush, churned by the killer hooves of contradictions.
My soul steams and smells like vegetation
after a sulphurous summer night of storms.
I get up, stand at the window: hollow, echoing sounds
from the town below, a baby's cry, an animal wailing.
Nightsmoke lies in the trees, reminding
me I am alone, how alone.
That sound I heard was the last tram flashing home
over the bridge, writing its sign in the rain.
And now, like someone slowly crossing the room,

a scythe taps on the wall . . . hallucinations!
I must lie down and rest. Sleep, so the nerves and brain
can heal. And the heart, the idiot heart.
My eyes burn, I can't sleep. And even if
  sleep comes, will tomorrow waken anything?

# *Part 2*

# *The Boy Changed into a Stag Clamours at the Gate of Secrets*

The mother called to her own son,
cried from far away,
the mother called to her own son,
cried from far away,
went to the front of the house: from there she cried,
unwound her heavy knot of hair
dusk wove to a shimmering bride's veil
that flowed down to her ankles
a flag, tasselled, black, for the wind
the firedamp dusk that smelled of blood.
She knotted her fingers to tendrils of stars,
the moon-froth covered her face,
and like this she cried to her dear son
as once she'd cried to her child –
stood in front of the house and spoke to the wind
spoke to the song-birds
to the love-cries of the wild geese
shouted across to the wind-fingered reeds
to the luminous sprawled potato-flower
to the stocky, cluster-balled bulls
to the sumach tree, shade of the well,
she called to the jumping fish
to the welding rings of water –
   Hush! you birds and branches
hush, because I'm calling
   be still, fishes and flowers
be still, I want to speak
   be quiet, breath of the soil
   fin-quiver, leafy parasols

be still, deep humming of sap
rumours that seep from the atoms' depths
   bronze-chaste virgins, wool-breasted flock
be quiet, because I'm calling,
I'm crying out to my own son!

      The mother called to her own son,
      the scream rose upward, writhing
      spiralling in the vortex of the universe –
      its blade glittered in the light
      like the scales of a spinning fish,
      like metal in roads, nitre in caves.
      The mother called to her own son:
come back, my dear son, come back
I am calling you, I, your own mother!
I am calling you, I, your river-bed
   I am calling you, your fountainhead
come back, my son, come back
   I call you, your memory's teat
come back, my son, come back
   I call you, your ragged tent
come back, my son, come back
   I call you, your guttering lamp.

Come back my son, I'm always knocking against things,
I have bruise-stains under my eyes, on the skin of my brow,
my calves, my thighs –
objects charge and butt me like angry rams,
the garden stake, chairs, the fence, gore me terribly,
doors thump me like Saturday drunkards,
the light's broken, the switch gives me shocks,
blood crawls in this skin of veins as through the beak of a
      stone-bruised bird,
   the scissors swim off like metal crabs,

matchsticks hop like sparrows' legs, the bucket handle hits
 back –
come back, my dear son, come back
I can no longer run like the young mother doe,
 my legs are ripe with bindweed,
 knotty, purplish roots grow in my thighs,
my toes swell with calcium-mounds,
 my fingers stiffen, with flesh tough as shell,
like snail's horn, scaly, like old shale-rock,
 my branches are sickly, dry and ready to snap –
come back, my son, come back
 for I'm spellbound,
 haggard, and full of visions –
 they flicker from my decaying glands
 as the winter morning cock-crow
pings off the frozen shirts hung on a fence –
I call you, your own mother
come back, my son, come back –
give meaning to all these things,
control them again: tame the knife,
 make the stubborn comb show itself,
for I'm just two green gritty eyes,
bubbles of light: like a dragonfly,
 which as you know, my child
 carries between its nape and jaw
two crystal apples that fill its whole skull,
I am two huge eyes without a face,
and their vision is not of this world.
Come back, my son, come back –
 breathe life into things again.

 The boy listened,
 he tossed his head,
 with nostrils like pails he

sniffed, his dewlap quivering –
his veined ears pricked at the sound
of that crying voice, his body tensed
as if sensing the hunter's footstep
or a whiff of smoke in the forest
when the smoke-blue forest
mourns its own burning, whimpering.
He swung his head that way
hearing the familiar voice cry,
suddenly stiffened with fear –
on his rump he noticed the fur,
discovered the split hooves,
stared at his cudweed shanks,
at his furry buck-apples
hidden there, where the lily shines.
He galloped across to a pool,
his chest ploughed through ferns,
body a muck of foam,
gouts of lather smacking the ground;
his four black hooves
stamp life from the flowers,
a tiny lizard is squashed, its
crushed neck-bib and tail grow cold.
He stoops over the pool,
stares into the moonlit water –
a beech-tree with the moon in its hair
shudders – the pool reflects a stag!
Then he sees that the thick fur
covers his body all over –
fur covers his knees and thighs,
his tassel-lipped penis sheath,
and antlers grow from his head
where the bone-branches have budded,
his face is furred to the chin,

the cut of his nostrils slanting in.
He whacks his antlers against a tree,
his neck a rope of veins,
paws the ground, his nerves strain
choking to bellow a cry –
but it's only the voice of a stag
his mother hears echoing back –
he'd weep the tears of a son,
and blows till the watery monster is gone,
blows, and in his breath's whirlpool
in the liquid midnight sparkle
little fishes with petal fins
scatter, their eyes like diamond-bubbles.
When the water's feathers settle again
it is a stag that stands in the moon-foam.

Now the boy shouted back
  bellowing, stretching his neck
the boy shouted back
  a stag's voice wildering through the fog –
mother, mother
I can't go back
mother, my mother
don't call me back
my nurse, my nurture
mother, mother
marvellous foaming spring
roof I grew up under
breasts with swollen buds
tent sheltering me from the frost
mother, my mother
don't ask me to come
mother, my mother
my one silky flower

my bird of gold
mother, mother,
don't call me back!
If I were to go back
my antlers would spear you,
my horns: tip to tip
I'd toss your old body –
if I were to go back
I'd tumble you on the ground
with these hooves I'd squash
your little breasts
my horns would stab you and stab
you, I'd bite you –
I'd trample your loins
if I went back
mother, mother
I'd rip you soul from body
bluebottles would flock to it –
the stars would gape
in shame at your soft lily-cleft,
though this gave me once
such lovely, tender warmth
in its lustre of oils,
warmth such as the breathing
cattle gave Jesus.
Mother, mother
you mustn't call me –
you'd turn to stone
you'd die, if you saw
your son coming.
Each branch of my horns
is a coil of gold rings
each twig of each branch
is a candlestick-cluster

each fang-sharp tip
is a fine funeral candle
each lace frond of horn
is a gold altar-cloth.
Believe me, you'd die
if you saw my sprawling
antlers filling the sky –
as on All Souls' Eve
the graveyard is lit
by candles, leaf by leaf,
my head is a petrified tree.
Mother, mother
if I found you
I'd scorch you to
a blackened stump,
I'd burn you to a lump
of greasy clay,
I'd roast you to chunks
of charred black meat.
Mother, mother
don't call to me –
if I went back
I'd eat you up
I'd wreck the house
with my thousand-tipped horns
I'd slash
the flowerbeds to pieces
I'd rip up the trees
with my stag's teeth
I'd swallow the well
in one gulp –
if I went back
I'd set fire to the house
then I'd gallop off

to the burial-plot
and with delicate nose
and all four hooves
I'd dig up my father –
I'd tear off the lid
of his coffin with my teeth –
I'd scatter his bones!
Mother, mother
don't call me back,
I can't go back.
If I did go back,
I would kill you.

So the boy cried with a stag's voice,
and the mother answered him,
come back, come back my son
I'm calling you, I, your own mother
come back, my son, come back
I'll cook you sour-cabbage soup, you can slice onion-rings into it,
they'll crunch in your teeth like bits of stone in a giant's jaws,
I'll give you warm milk in a clean glass,
in my cellar the lair of fire-bellied frogs
in my cellar blinking like a giant green toad
I'll gently pour wine into heron-necked bottles,
with my stony fists I'll knead bread – for I know, I know
how to bake round little froth-bellied loaves, and Sunday twists-
come back, come back my son
I plucked the crops of live, shrieking geese for your feather bed,
I cried I plucked the geese cried . . . the feather-wounds drooled white fat,

I sunned your straw mattress, I shook it out,
the clean-swept courtyard is listening for you, the table is
laid.

Aiii mother, mother
I cannot go back,
don't give me your twists of milk-loaf
or sweet goat's milk in a flowered glass
Don't make my bed springy and soft
or pluck out the throats of the geese –
throw the wine away, pour it over your father's grave,
weave the onions into a wreath,
fry your frothy doughnuts for the little ones now.
For the warm milk would turn to vinegar in my
mouth,
a stone would squat in place of the milk loaf,
the wine in my glass would turn to blood,
each soft bed-feather become a flame,
the small drinking mug a blade of blue sword-lily.
Aiii mother, aiii, aiii mother –
I can't go back to my birthplace now.
Only the green forest can hold me,
the house is too small for my huge, furry horns,
the courtyard has no space for my graveyard antlers,
the shaking world-tree of my branching antlers
with stars as its leaves, the Milky Way as its moss.
I can only eat sweet-smelling grass,
the tender young grass is my cud –
I can no longer drink from a flowered glass,
only from a spring, only from a clean, fresh spring!

I don't understand, I don't understand your strange talk, son
you speak with a stag's voice, the soul of a stag moves in
you, my poor one.

When the turtle dove weeps, turtle dove weeps, the little bird calls, little bird calls, my son
why am I, why am I in all creation the unhappy one?
Do you still remember, still remember your little mother, my son?
I don't understand, I don't understand your piteous crying, son.
Do you remember how happily you'd come running home, with your school-report,
you dissected frogs, nailed their speckled webby hands to the fence,
lost yourself in your airplane books, helped me in with the washing?
You were in love with Irena B. . . . V. J., and H. S. the painter, his beard like a wild orchid, was your friend.
Do you still remember, Saturday nights when your father came home sober, how happy you were?

Aiii, mother, mother, don't remind me. My sweetheart and friends,
they swam from me cold like fish. The poppy-throated painter,
who knows where he went, mother – where my youth went?
Mother, mother don't mention my father. Sorrow flowers, blossoms from his flesh of earth. Don't mention my father –
he'll get up from his grave, gather up his yellow bones
and come staggering out – his nails, his hair sprouting again.
Aiii, aiii! Old Wilhelm came, the coffin-maker, runt with a doll's face.
He said, I'll grab your feet, we'll put you nicely into the box –

but I started retching with fear. I'd just come back from Pest,
you used to go there too, by train . . . a caretaker . . . the rails got twisted.
Aiii, I'd have cut myself to pieces, the candle puddling shadows on your taut face –
Latzi, our new brother-in-law, the barber, shaved you. The candles drooled like babies,
their innards melting out, dribbles, the bowels gleaming, the nerves shining through.
The Choral Society stood around in their purple caps, lowing your death like cattle,
and I touched your forehead. Your hair was alive,
I heard it grow, saw the bristles beginning on your chin –
by morning your chin was black, next day your throat was spiky like stalks of viper's bugloss,
a slice of hairy melon, a yellow caterpillar with a blue-cabbage skin.
Aiii, I thought it would outgrow the room, the courtyard, the whole world
your beard and hair, the stars in it humming like vermin.
Aiii, aiii! In the dense green of rain, the red horses pulling your hearse whinnied in fear –
one kicked out at your head, the other pissed helplessly, its purple
cunt flopped out like a hanged man's tongue, the coachman swore,
rain washed the blare of the brass band, your mates were blowing and sobbing,
stood blowing by the thorny, thistled chapel wall,
blew out a basket of silvery breath from their puffed black lips,
blew the tune with cracked bloody lips and bloodshot eyes,

blew the card games, wines-and-sodas, the bloated and
    withered women,
blew the minted planets of coins, baksheesh, up into the
    void after you,
blew the thick dust of hopelessness away, sobbing. The
    tune
blared from the hard, glinting, O-mouthed horns into a
    void stinking of corpses –
petrified loves, decaying women, the mouldering militias
    of grandfathers,
cottages, cradles, enamel and silver onion pocket-
    watches,
Easter bells multiplying redeemers like a bird's wing
    fanning,
trumpeting briefcases, train-wheels, brass-buttoned
    ratings stiff with salutes.
They blew with gum-pink teeth, the friends, with black
    puffy liver lips,
and you led them: That's it, lads! That's great! Aiii, don't
    stop playing –
your hands, crossed, a pair of gold spiders, long legs,
    jointed, hinged spokes of your heart.
Your shoes in the cupboard wait for the next-of-kin, your
  breadcrust-callous feet look childlike, helpless in their
  white socks,
and your mates blew on in the dashing rain, the trumpet-
    stops hiccupped like steel adam's apples,
like claws of the reptile-bird, Carcharodon's teeth, the
    brass trumpets glittered.
Aiii, mother, mother, don't speak of my father.
Leave him be, his eyes stare from the earth like buds.

The mother called to her own son,
cried, from far away

come back my son, come back
  come away from that stone world
stag of the stone forest, smogs, electric grids and neon
    glitter.
  The iron bridges and tramlines, they thirst for your blood,
    a hundred times a day they jab you, but you never hit
    back –
  I am calling you, I, your own mother
    come back my son, come back.

There he stood on the crest of all time,
there he stood on creation's highest mountain,
there he stood at the gate of secrets –
the points of his antlers played with the stars
and with a stag's voice he cried,
cried back to the mother who'd borne him –
  mother, mother, I can't go back
the hundred wounds in me weep pure gold,
I die every day, a hundred bullets in me
every day I get up again a hundred times stronger
I die every day three billion deaths
and three billion times a day I am born,
each prong of my antlers a twin-legged pylon
each branch of my antlers a high-tension wire,
my eyes are ports of cargo-ships, my veins are greased cables,
my teeth are iron bridges, my heart is a thrashing ocean of
    monsters,
each vertebra is a thriving city, my spleen is a chuffing stone-
    barge,
each cell is a vast factory, every atom a solar system,
my testicles are the sun and moon, the Milky Way is my
    spine-marrow,
each point in space is one grain of my body,
each galaxy an inkling of my brain.

Son, my lost son, I still want you back –
your mother's eyes, like a dragonfly's, won't rest until
you come.

To die I'll come back, only to die.
To die I'll come back,
mother – only to die will I come.
Then you can lay me out in my childhood home,
with your age-veined hands you can wash my body,
close my eyelids, swollen glands, with kisses.
And when the flesh falls off me,
and the stench it was sweetens to flowers,
I'll be a foetus drinking your blood,
I'll be your little boy again –
and this hurts only you, mother,
aiii, hurts only you, mother.

# *Part 3*

## *Hunger and Hate*

If there were a god I'd deny him.
I'd hammer the dead flesh of his face.
I'd snap at his hand like a dog as he stooped
to pat me. With tears and a gun I'd waylay him.

I'd take a rainbow-quick sliver
of glass, and gouge his balls out.
I'd slash at his groin till the pain
was red-hot and his blood gushed rust like oil.

I'd gnaw at his shinbone
with its spidery hairs, a mad dog
foaming away the obedient centuries –

then I'd yank his heart out, like the shark
biting through all the ages of fish on the hook –
a greasy stomach, a mottled blue fin.

## *Four Seasons*

Autumn is gone. The leaves have turned to mould.
I tramped over the mush of plants on my way to you.
My orphaned eyes skulked in holes the dead had abandoned
like hermit crabs in the dead shells they crawl to.
The whale-mouthed iron railings dribbled violet shadows of the dead,
spongy babies, stale chrysanthemums, hung from their lips, moaning and crying.
They brought me a blue turtle dove, a gold chain and a bell on its tiny leg.
I drowned in your atom-splitting smile, your moongaze turned my hair grey.

And winter's over. Not like winters we knew.
A sky of bone crackles in the jaws of the church bells.
Teeth chattering like machine-guns I went out begging crumbs for you.
The still forest glittered like broken glass.
Shadows blue as hyacinth blurred from the frosted railings,
and grieving, hooded in quiet, the animals, tip-toeing, circled your window.
By the bed I listened to your breezy chatter, like a jasmin rustling,
and red deer, hare, pheasant, thrush, heard the white flame of your song in the churned snow.

And now it is spring. A soft mould-flush
oozes and sticks to the walls in a thin green glaze.
Dead flower-heads drift and soak in the jelly mush,
and death circles in from the void, misting the eyes.
The blotchy railings vomit bile-green shadows
where maneating fish and stars with shark's teeth swirl
home to the feast,
brought by sick lusts and stale prayers, mad gibberings
and curses.
And I, an elder tree on your deadalive grave, throw my-
self on the stelae of your breasts.

Summer will come, minting us gold with light.
On the moon the magic unicorn rears with his
blue grin.
And the wailing world remembers its griefs, the
nerves tensing around it.
In its ultraviolet scum, the insect breeds to dis-
traction;
acid shadows drip from the peeling railings,
and butterflies burn to ash on your heart, as the lizard's
fist squeezes it.
In this garden of ferns I hear your girl-flower
weeping.
In this cave of blood-red stones I moan to you, a black
leopard buried alive in your heart.

## *The Flower of Silence*

The flower of silence fades to grief's huge funeral leaves
Don't cry don't scream don't tear me apart with your eyes
Don't tie me to the grieving cross with live ropes weeping
  blood
I'm drying up my flesh my glands death is a shimmer of flies

My nerve-tentacles weave through the dripping stars
Squeezing and sucking the blood of starfish I'm drunk
I'm a mad green eye whirled on the poles of its grief
Help me my carnivore mask has eaten away my face

Go back to the forest I heard the song of the stag
Silence is every leaf the trees grow noiselessly
Peace is a wandering doe the birds are scarlet flowers
My heart seed of your heart the flower of silence opens.

# *A Church in Bulgaria*

Inside a church in Batak in 1876, 4,000 Bulgarians were massacred by the Turks.

Wreathed into the earth, a stone coffin, this church,
an unbreakable stone bubble:
it wants to flutter away, soar in the air
but is torn by its dead weight down into the soil –
earth gnaws at its solid mass
through the spidery roots which suckle it too.
Like a horse's skull stripped of its glory of flesh,
the past! a grinning skull
which the humus hasn't buried quite –
humus, the earth, the oval cropland
which whirls with us, rolls in the burning dust of space.
And what's kept there, hoarded
deep, as in men's hearts? What's buried there,
dragged down into itself incalculable
millions of years: silence which won't complain?
Bone, vertebra, skull, self-sweat,
metal, coal and fern;
earth's earliest beasts crystallized in unknown layers,
flowers of the far past, fish cut in stone,
old anthems, shards of forgotten epics
and again: bone, vertebra, skull,
whole millennia of flaking eyes,
prehistoric fish-rot, gases, oils,
statues the marble limbs of dead cities
lost in the stale and fresh strata, they jab at the earth from
 beneath;

and lava, the liquid fire earth spews at will.
This seeps from the earth, earth dries it, like sweat on a
  thinking head,
or a mammoth brain its own thoughts,
time without end.

Earth I stand on, here, bloodsoaked stones
I won't pry deeper, or ask more of your past.
The lesson is here, in the blood-ruined beams
of this stone skull blown by man's brain, walls clenched
    under its weight
like old men's shoulders already bending
under, to earth. There they'll fall. Where the stones grew
was man's source too: he was cast up from it
like the fish from water. Above him the dust tides over
unruffled, still: just rolls with a smothering rumble.

For they're here too: bones, vertebrae, skulls, a yellow
heap in the marble coffin's belly of mirrors* –
bones, vertebrae, skulls. Look, like a lime-bubble
or water-bead: white bones with a baby's head,
or an old man's, like a black sod,
a tiny shinbone, knotty and yellow and
hollow like a straw; a carious, fat
starshape vertebra, twisted fingerbones,
a skull drilled with bullet-holes
like a maggoty fruit, a virgin's delicate
knotted kneecap, like a walking stick – all one spiky heap
like a hayrick pitched over stakes out on a lake.
For the coffin's reflecting belly of mirrors
flashes one lesson a thousand ways –
bone, vertebra, skull.

* *Note:* The custom of placing the bones of saints in mirror-lined coffins occurs in the Greek Orthodox Church.

What happened here? What does this crying emblem
mean, here in the heart of the church this once-
soul and marrow-gifted crown?
It mourns the madness of power, greed, pride – and the
    dignity
of defiance, passion of man and woman,
for you, you earth, the fiery unquenchable core in us
  Liberty!

The defiance whose eyes would drill through rock
rather than smile for dictators.
Man's stubbornness is such
he'd sooner gnash his tongue to a bloody
spittle than thank his oppressors.
And the courage: woman who'd show her full white breasts
like the Carpathian heights under snow,
as a mocking gift to the knives christian or
infidel – but cries 'Be damned to you, murderer!'
And the honour, this hairy male-breast
more muscular than the chest of a horse, he
bares to their guns, steel weaker than his gaze.

Here the blood rose high as their heads, trembling –
dome and window moist with its ruby steam,
in this church, the eye of a dragonfly husk.
Here it stood, a black jelly of fear,
the slaughtered patriots' blood –
men, women and children who stood
silently frowning, victims watching
this blood-rampage of power.
For the human heart endures much
but can't live in its iron bands forever –
suddenly it flares up like a dying star,
anger gushing energy in a shower of fire.

Which is what these did: the downtrodden
raised their arms and eyes against the oppressor.

O he knew already the game was over,
the trick lost, the dice gone dead in his hand!
So before he'd crouch terrified over the horse's mane
and escape on the stallion flying with swollen nostrils and veins
sweating crimson froth, he held,
here, a last feast, a human pig-killing.
For still he craved flesh, lusted to be drunk
on the steaming crimson broth, that magic stallion.
Drop by drop he filled the stone communion cup with blood.
This blood-guzzling, this stony eucharist, is history now.

The seared villages, fired huts,
virgins spitted on swords, women
with marble skins ripped by diamond spear-holes,
broken lilies, gouged eyes
weeping like squashed plums –
these visions, like the mica-flakes of the Milky Way
remain, to haunt the child of a later century.
As here, now: the bones, vertebrae, skulls, heaped up
holy reminder and lesson,
in this church shocked to stone.
Bones, vertebrae, skulls . . . enough.
Can my senses still live with this sight,
this heaped imagery of horror?
Is there one cell left in my body
which hasn't suffered the death these bones did?

Is there a cell in my brain
that isn't part of this grandeur now?

Have you an ounce of shame left,
poet? Shame for yourself
as you stand here, in a white shirt, a summer suit,
on the stones of this church in August '52?

# *A Message Too Late*

I read your poems again, my friend.
I read them slowly, line by line,
thumbing the pages, thinking of you, my friend.
And why deny it? I wept at the thought of your name.
I wasn't sorting them, sheep from goats
like a mustering of autumn conscripts –
I just gave up and stared at the massed rows
of your poems, your whole identity, friend.
Here your dry X-ray sight opens
the cave-dwellers' lair, and the flowers of doubt,
and the wings of the pterodactyl, flesh-eater, bird-father,
to get at the secrets of the human heart.
Like the surgeon in Rembrandt's picture
you showed us dissection, you raped a dead world's nerves.
How you must have sweated days,
bringing those nightmare facts to life!
Hunched over the corpse's rainbow guts
by the light of the smelly oil-lamp in your cellar,
your dry obsession made your fingers itch –
but in the end, what can a corpse tell you?
Well it's here, we see it. You forced us to see.
Now what will cleanse the infection from our eyes?
You never forgave us our wrongheadedness –
but is there no hope? Not one refreshing word?
Just one word as clear as the rain
that gives birth to a homeland or curses a world?

# *Black Peacock*

Points, angles, hollows, lines, all
meet in this head: rough-chiselled, its veins still showing.
The eye is ringed with a deep
moat of sadness, a trench hammered out of tin.

Remember, Pishta, the winter nights would cry –
'Even Jesus shouldered his own green tree!
Someone's kissing Pishta's girl, and it isn't he!'

Lurching like an old gravestone,
he rubs against the nudging shoulders of women.
His tears are knives with mother-of-pearl handles.
His words kindle timeless shivers under their skin.

Pishta, old friend, remember when we sat
on the Danube embankment, on top of that marble post,
and love wailed and cried like something lost.

He has no father or mother.
Perhaps God dreamed him up
to ease his own conscience. But when he turns
to dust the Phoenix is born, the snowdrop opens.

Remember, Pishta, remember
the sky was a wireless bringing us news, it was winter,
we wept: can one still kiss and play the lover?

On his heart a black peacock struts and cries.
Talk to him . . . he lurches away, won't answer.
Won't talk, but listens for the peacock step.
Does nothing but cry, in the spell of the peacock's cry.

Remember, Pishta, old friend of mine,
those days when love was like a bottle of wine,
a moonlit track cutting through snow and pine.

Girls, don't tear him to pieces
like convicts squabbling over a loaf of bread.
Griefs, don't rant and scrabble around him
like furies over the heart of a dying man.

Pishta, remember the other day
I swore I would let myself waste away
if I didn't find my life's share of joy?

Now those who can love, and kill for love,
have time enough to hate him,
if from this bundle of points, angles, hollows
and lines, only silence, numbness, is left of him.

# *The Rainbow-Coloured Whale*

Now your grave is sinking,
like your back
when the scalpel
cut away your ribs.

They say, the wreath
we laid at your head has withered,
the plank's gone rotten
that propped your dead heart.

Your grave is sinking deeper,
a black mouth lying in wait.
Every day I bring fresh earth
in a big willow basket.

But the earth I bring in the evening
is gone by morning;
the earth I bring in the morning
by nightfall has sunk without trace.

As if you were eating
and eating your way through the earth,
forever upwards,
with those toothless gums.

The salt-spray eating the coral
becomes the coral –
the worm devoured you,
now you devour the worm.

You eat through it all
like a huge grub,
insatiable mouth without stomach,
munching into daylight.

Tons of stones and clay –
nothing can stop those jaws!
What can you want in our world
with your dead will?

Skull, Nothing,
what is it you want?
Learn the final lesson.
You are alone now.

Rainbow-coloured whale,
swimming the waters under the earth,
obey the laws of the earth,
the vows of death and burial.

Earth swallowed you whole,
and you swallowed the whole world.
No hope, no body left –
it's time you understood.

Rainbow-coloured whale, thrashing and
churning the clogged waters under the earth,
you are a predator now,
not worthy of what you were.

When you were alive your skin
was a breathing marsh of colours,
your sweat gushed in little
squirts, like hypodermics.

But you haven't noticed
how naked you've grown,
how the black earth
has melted you.

Those cold eyes that knew
the stone-green world of boulder and pine
have burst by now,
soft, like sea-weed pods.

You didn't even know
they'd betrayed you –
sold every ounce of you
for Judas-gold!

The traces left in the air
by your wandering desires –
gone forever,
under the hoarfrost.

And whatever sediment remained
of your heart
has been turned to stone,
melted away with the waters.

Little by little
time has eaten
the tartar from your teeth,
the grief from your eyes.

And it's time you learnt
not to see hope in such signs.
When a man dies,
he loses his will to live.

My grief for you was like thorns,
but the thorns have withered.
The green tree of your absence
is slowly beginning to flower.

The tusks of the black boar,
the tusks of the black boar that
slashed you open –
the sting has gone out of the wound.

But why were you never
as hungry as this –
so hungry I feel you
unwinding out of the grave?

No man has the right
to live it all over again!
I haven't the strength
to bury you twice!

Look, your sea's dried up –
don't thrash about
in the earth's black surf
as if it were water.

You'd swallow the sun
like a goldfish?
Strain the sumach tree
through your teeth, like parsley?

Bone-flower,
burrowing towards the light,
don't ever blossom. Don't gnaw
into our moonlight with your rat's teeth.

Larva,
don't eat your way into my heart.
I live with your absence.
You don't exist.

Life here is peaceful
without you.
Flower then, flower into
the death-wish of the lily.

## *Thursday, Day of Superstition*

On the third day it is hardest, on the third.

Distracted, nowhere to go,
I roam this island of stone and neon, the Octagon.
It is Thursday evening,
no time for cursing,
no time for crying.

Red, blue, yellow, green, the rain is falling.
The streets are rainbows
riddled with pattering bubbles.
The bubble-creatures roll their eyes
like chameleons, round and round
as a pebble rolls in a clay jar.
Their watery skins
ripple from colour to colour –
the lizards of rain crawl all over each other.
This island is Galapagos,
this lonely flowering of stones.

I am alone.

The island spins like a huge merry-go-round.
Taxis, buses, trams – step up for the joy-ride!
The shop-fronts whirl round and round like drunken stars.
The sword-lilies are whores in this amusement park.

Red, blue, yellow, green, the rain is falling.
The news-vendors are shouting.
The flower-sellers say nothing.

To the rooftops, silent, glowing,
animal-flowers are climbing the scaffolding –
night's instant creatures,
the neon monsters.

My heart sees its fate crucified on the sky –
a twinkling map of neon,
a huge technicolour brain,
Hungary.

Its villages, its towns,
brain cells, needles of light,
electric rivers of blue veins,
convolutions of land and brain.

## I'M LOSING MY MIND!

On the third day it is hardest, on the third.

No time for cursing.
No time for crying.

But the rain is flowering a roof,
patches of wall, a hint of sky where
a tiny spider of light hangs in its web of light.
And through the dripping light-cells crawls
the mimosa leaf of advertisements,
opening, twirling, closing
like a sea-anemone's head . . .
slowly it sways,
feeling its way.

## HELP ME SOMEONE!

But through the dripping rain-
ferns, monsters are crawling . . .
nylon, plastic and rubber
skins, hiss
and crackle and shine in the light as they move.

Women in lizard skins.
Men in snake skins.

They hunger.
And they thirst.

A bestiary
of red, blue, green and yellow faces.

Who knows me standing here in the cold?
Who will accept my gift of flowers?
Who are my friends? Where have they gone?
My voice is a shout in a dream.

I search the rain,
looking for you.
A blue voice calling you, calling you.

From the red, yellow and green
scribbles of light,
night sketches a shape in the rain –
a giant beer mug.
It has just a minute to live.

The amber beer sparkles like fire.
Neon lather slops over the rim

vomiting, dribbling yellow stains
of frothing electricity into the rain.

Where am I going?
What song am I singing?

'Save me, O Lord, from all evil'

On the third day it is hardest, on the third.

What am I doing here?
Where else is there?

I flounder around in the swill of neon beer.
But I feel like a child wanting to scream,
to be given something . . . and how the world would laugh!
O Hungary I'd climb the neon veins of your body and skull,
I'd sprawl on your neon brain
so the world could see in radiance through my ribs
my beating heart's blister,
your own heart.

No, it is not permitted.

On the third day it is hardest, on the third.

No time for cursing,
no time for weeping.
In this wilderness of rainbow and rain
I hear my grandmother's voice again –
'Save me, Lord, from the unicorn, the four-breasted bird
Save me, Lord, from the mangy ram and the whinneying
flower

Save me, Lord, from the barking toad and the hooved angel
Save me O Lord, save me from all evil'

But who's there? Who am I talking to?
Who can save himself with a song?
I denied God. I laughed him away.
I flicked his balls with thorns and ran like a street-boy.
I've blown my tiny flame
to a tree of fire, ten miles high –
and the scorched insects fall like ash from the sky.
Red, blue, green,
I wear as my laurels this neon wreath,
I drown in the purple beard of a neon man
whose tentacles lick through my skull to devour the brain.

Only you can save me, you.
On the third day it is hardest, on the third.

What do I want?
What did I ever want?
I dug myself into your heart
like a soldier, numbed by the shells,
deeper and deeper into the mud of your heart
under the grinning jack o' lantern
skulls, and the shrapnel leafing like trees
all around me . . . flies dabbing the blood
from the rags and swaying vines of flesh and veins
and rainbow lids and eyes twitching like flowers.

I lie curled
like a question, an embryo,
in the drumming jungle of your blood.
Your ribs sway softly like a crib,
but your heavy heartbeat shakes me,

the pulse and clutch of your entrails shakes me.
I hear the cauldron of your liver,
the sweat of your kidneys dripping phosphor;
my eye is the risen moon in your night,
its tentacles probing
for dawn in the dark of your body.
You are the depths of space and ocean to me.

I'm alone.

You are with me.

Red, blue, yellow, green . . .
still the rain is falling.
The sea is swirling full of phosphorus eyes.
The sea's brain, Hungary,
is a neon medusa drifting above me,
and our world, an anemone lost in the chaos of space
swims round and round in a gulf of the Milky Way.

Larva,
I know you'll shed your skin.
Your gift is flight. You will begin
stretching your frail new amber wings,
unfurling them from their glues of birth,
and their fibres will dry in the warm wind
as the wings flutter, fanning free of the blue slime –
and the womb of time will close behind
you. I know, because our fates are the same.

I'm alone.
I bow my rainsoaked head.

On the third day it is hardest, on the third.
It is Thursday evening,

no time for cursing,
no time for weeping.

Hell-bent on life, like a sponge, I head for home
in the red, green and blue rain: in the age of socialism.

# *More about Penguins*

*Penguinews*, which appears every month, contains details of all the new books issued by Penguins as they are published. From time to time it is supplemented by *Penguins in Print*, which is a complete list of all books published by Penguins which are in print. (There are well over three thousand of these.)

A specimen copy of *Penguinews* will be sent to you free on request, and you can become a subscriber for the price of the postage. For a year's issues (including the complete lists) please send 4s. if you live in the United Kingdom, or 8s. if you live elsewhere. Just write to Dept EP, Penguin Books Ltd, Harmondsworth, Middlesex, enclosing a cheque or postal order, and your name will be added to the mailing list.

Some other Poetry books published by Penguins are described on the following pages.

Note: *Penguinews* and *Penguins in Print* are not available in the U.S.A. or Canada

# *Children of Albion*

## POETRY OF THE 'UNDERGROUND' IN BRITAIN

*Edited by Michael Horovitz*

Here at last is the 'secret' generation of British poets whose work could hitherto be discovered only through their own bush telegraph of little magazines and lively readings. These are the energies which have almost completely dispelled the arid critical climate of the 'fifties' and engineered a fresh renaissance of 'the voice of the bard' –

The anthology contains many of the best poems of

Pete Brown, Dave Cunliffe, Roy Fisher, Lee Harwood, Spike Hawkins, Anselm Hollo, Bernard Kops, Tom McGrath, Adrian Mitchell, Edwin Morgan, Neil Oram, Tom Pickard, Tom Raworth, Chris Torrance, Alex Trocchi, Gael Turnbull

– and *fifty* others – from John Arden to Michael X –

It is edited by Michael Horovitz, with a Blakean cornucopia of 'afterwords' which trace the development of oral and jazz poetry – the Albert Hall Incarnation of 1965 – the influences of the great American and Russian spokesmen – and the diverse lyric, political, visioning and revolutionary orientations of these new poets.

## *British Poetry Since 1945*

*Edited with an Introduction by Edward Lucie-Smith*

*British Poetry Since 1945* is the first largely comprehensive anthology of poetry written during this period in England, Scotland, Wales and Northern Ireland. The anthology is arranged to show how the various styles and manners current during the quarter of a century under review relate to one another. Critical notes on as many as 83 poets that are represented, and on their work, as well as bibliographies of each poet's main books make this anthology an ideal introduction to recent British poetry. For those readers already familiar with the field, *British Poetry Since 1945* will prove an invaluable source of reference.

## *Hugh MacDiarmid Selected Poems*

*Selected and edited by David Craig and John Manson*

This book aims to make more readily available a comprehensive selection from the work of a poet who exacts attention on the same level as the accepted masters of modern poetry. For although MacDiarmid was working at the highest level from the early 20s to the later 30s, most of his work has been available in very limited editions, and some not published at all. In his more complex and fluent philosophical poetry, such as *By Wauchopeside* and *Water of Life*, and in such poems as *The Seamless Garment* and *Lo! A Child is Born*, he is at least the equal of Auden and Yeats. For those readers unfamiliar with literary or spoken Scots, a useful glossary of the most difficult words has been added at the foot of each page.

# *Penguin Modern European Poets*

*Apollinaire*

SELECTED POEMS

Guillaume Apollinaire was a friend and supporter of the Cubists. His own experimental poetic forms employ rhythms which dispense with punctuation and a style of typography derived from exercises on postcards sent from the front in the First World War. Yet he is also the last of the poets in France whose lines young people know by heart.

*Yevtushenko*

SELECTED POEMS

Yevgeny Yevtushenko is the fearless spokesman of his generation in Russia. In verse that is young, fresh, and outspoken he frets at restraint and injustice, as in his now famous protest over the Jewish pogrom at Kiev. But he can write lyrically, too, of the simple things of humanity – love, a birthday, a holiday in Georgia. And in 'Zima Junction' he brilliantly records his impressions on a visit to his home in Siberia.

*Zbginiew Herbert*

SELECTED POEMS

No country has suffered more of the brutalities of Communism and Fascism than Poland. Yet Zbigniew Herbert, the most classical of its poets, is neither nationalist nor Catholic. He speaks for no party. *Avant-garde* in manner, but controlled, precise, and honest in thought, he stands aside from the chaos all around him, ironically bent on survival. His is the voice of sanity.

# *Penguin Modern European Poets*

*Günter Grass*

POEMS OF GÜNTER GRASS

Günter Grass, famous as a novelist, is here presented as a poet in a selection from his three published volumes. Grass's belief that an artist, however committed he may be in life, should be only a jester in art, is admirably practised in these poems in which fantasy, ingenuity and humour are substitutes for didacticism, and no word, thing or idea is too sacrosanct to be played with. Even in the recent controversial political poems, which come close to blurring his division between life and art, Grass's tremendous zest and sensuous response are felt.

*Eugenio Montale*

SELECTED POEMS

Since the publication of *Ossi di Seppia*, his first volume of poems, in 1925, Eugenio Montale has come to be seen in Italy as 'the poet' of this century. His reputation is now international.

Truth is the only star Montale has followed. Leaning neither to the right nor the left, favouring neither the Catholic church nor the Communist party, he has stood on his own and kept his perception completely clear. His poetry can be difficult, even obscure, but frequently it reflects life in a strong, musical diction which has been compared to that of T. S. Eliot.

## *Penguin Books of Verse*

*The Penguin Book of Animal Verse*
*The Penguin Book of Chinese Verse*
*The Penguin Book of Contemporary Verse*
*The Penguin Book of Elizabethan Verse*
*The Penguin Book of Romantic English Verse*
*The Penguin Book of English Verse*
*The Penguin Book of French Verse*
(Three Volumes)
*The Penguin Book of German Verse*
*The Penguin Book of Irish Verse*
*The Penguin Book of Italian Verse*
*The Penguin Book of Japanese Verse*
*The Penguin Book of Restoration Verse*
*The Penguin Book of Russian Verse*
*The Penguin Book of Satirical Verse*
*The Penguin Book of Scottish Verse*
*The Penguin Book of Sick Verse*
*The Penguin Book of South African Verse*
*The Penguin Book of Spanish Verse*
*The Penguin Book of Twentieth-Century German Verse*
*The Penguin Book of Victorian Verse*
*The Penguin Book of Welsh Verse*

# *The Penguin Modern Poets*

All the earlier volumes in this series are still available. The more recent volumes are:

THE PENGUIN MODERN POETS 6
George MacBeth, Edward Lucie-Smith, and Jack Clemo

THE PENGUIN MODERN POETS 7*
Richard Murphy, Jon Silkin, and Nathaniel Tarn

THE PENGUIN MODERN POETS 8*
Edwin Brock, Geoffrey Hill, and Stevie Smith

THE PENGUIN MODERN POETS 9†
Denise Levertov, Kenneth Rexroth, and William Carlos Williams

THE PENGUIN MODERN POETS 10
Adrian Henri, Roger McGough, and Brian Patten

THE PENGUIN MODERN POETS 11
D. M. Black, Peter Redgrove, and D. M. Thomas

THE PENGUIN MODERN POETS 12*
Alan Jackson, Jeff Nuttall, and William Wantling

THE PENGUIN MODERN POETS 13
Charles Bukowski, Philip Lamantia, and Harold Norse

THE PENGUIN MODERN POETS 14
Alan Brownjohn, Michael Hamburger, and Charles Tomlinson

THE PENGUIN MODERN POETS 15
Alan Bold, Edward Brathwaite, and Edwin Morgan

THE PENGUIN MODERN POETS 16
Jack Beeching, Harry Guest, and Matthew Mead

THE PENGUIN MODERN POETS 17
W. S. Graham, Kathleen Raine, and David Gascoyne

**Not for sale in the U.S.A.*
*†Not for sale in the U.S.A. or Canada*